TESTIMONIALS

"*Toxic Bosses* explains toxic leaders with examples and illustrations and elaborates with the unethical organizations that fell from grace. It offers tips, tools, and techniques to excel as ethical leaders. It is a well-researched book on ethical and moral leadership. I strongly recommend reading this book."—**Professor M.S. Rao, Ph.D.**, #1 Thought Leader and Influencer on Culture Globally by Thinkers 360

"Once again, Ray hits the visionary high note with his expert insights and practical wisdom around Toxic Bosses. If you've ever had a toxic board member, advisor, senior or executive-level boss and are bewildered by their behavior, get this book!"—**Stephanie Frank, CVO,** The Holisec Group and author of 4x International Best Selling Author of *The Accidental Millionaire.*

"Ray's well-thought out and well-researched book covers the damage caused by unethical leaders in organizations, what organizations can do to correct this, and what we can do to protect ourselves. It's a fascinating read for anyone in business today as we all need to raise our awareness on this topic to be able to support building moral and ethical cultures within organizations."—**Mike Desjardins, CEO,** ViRTUS Inc., leadership training company.

TOXIC

BOSSES

Practical Wisdom for Developing Wise, Ethical and Moral Leaders

---

Ray Williams

Toxic Bosses: Practical Wisdom for Developing Wise, Ethical and Moral Leaders

Includes bibliographical references.

ISBN: 9798709430716

1. Ethical. 2. Moral. 3. Toxic. 4. Leaders. 4 Wisdom

Note: The names, details and circumstances may have been changed to protect the privacy of those mentioned in this publication. This publication is not intended as a substitute for the advice of health care individuals.

DEDICATION

For my wife, partner and friend,

Diane, in gratitude for her

inspiration and never-ending support.

And for my father, Brinley Williams, a man of exquisite
ethics, morality and wisdom.

ACKNOWLEDGMENTS

M y deepest appreciation goes to my wife, Diane Williams, for editing this book in detail, providing valuable suggestions and supporting me in all ways in this project.

My appreciation also goes to Mike Desjardins, an inspirational, wise and ethical leader and CEO of ViRTUS, a leading edge Vancouver-based leadership development company, for his insights, suggestions and support in reviewing the manuscript.

Gratitude to my friend and colleague Stephanie Frank, builder of 2 multi-million dollar businesses; holder of 15 technical and behavioral certifications in the fields of Cyber Intelligence, Large Scale Systems Design, Facial Expression, Neurolinguistics, Positive Psychology and Personality Profiling; and author of 4x International Best Selling Author of *The Accidental Millionaire* for her outstanding suggestions for refocusing my message and book promotion

TABLE OF CONTENTS

PREFACE

I have written this book because I am deeply concerned about the chaos developing in the world and the absence and decline of wise, moral and ethical leaders, particularly in America.

We have experienced dark and difficult times before in our history—World Wars, the Depression, and pandemics, but the physical, political and economic health of nations is now overlaid with the potentially catastrophic effects of climate change.

While it may seem like I'm an alarmist, I do have a historical perspective of dark times, having been a prisoner of war during WWII, so my observations and conclusions are not reached lightly or without context.

My perspective too is one from the latter stages of my career and life which have allowed me to reflect on the nature of the world that will be left for my children and grandchildren. Without dramatic, sustained changes in who we choose as leaders and the standards we hold them to, the future of democracy will be dark.

My hope is that this book can serve as a useful reference for both reflection and the necessary action that is necessary to lift us, our institutions and organizations out of the current chaotic situation.

INTRODUCTION

We live in a world fraught with ecological and social problems and political systems that diminish democracy. We have organizations that demean and dehumanize many of their employees, and an economic perspective that places material wealth and financial interests over social, ecological, and human interests. Such a system devalues what it means to be human, compromising the inherent dignity and worth of people who are not at the top, not to mention devaluing the worth of non-human living beings, including the Earth itself.

Our world cries out for moral, ethical and wise leadership that recognizes and honors the dignity of all living beings, and makes decisions in the interest of society and the planet for now and the future.

Looking at the state of the world today, one cannot help but wonder what we need to do to ensure a positive and peaceful future for humanity. How is it possible that knowledge and information have become so much more accessible to people, but we do not seem to have become any wiser?

We continue to destroy our natural habitat despite ominous warnings of the planet becoming uninhabitable. We continue to be led by dictators and autocrats despite the many lessons from history of the incredible damage they can cause. We continue to allow without correction racial and ethnic injustice and increasing economic and income inequality. We continue to allow the amoral, unethical behaviors of our leaders (and their followers) with no, or few consequences. Even worse, we continue to recruit and promote into leadership positions narcissists, sociopaths and psychopaths.

Unrestrained and unchecked, the result is the degradation of moral standards, ethical behavior and the decline of democracy.

This book examines the connection between moral and ethical leaders and wisdom. Our current turbulent and dangerous times underscores the need to have wise leaders who demonstrate the highest standards of moral principles and ethical behavior. While all countries are in need of wise, moral and ethical leaders, nowhere does it have greater impact on the world than in the United States.

This book is organized into three major sections. The first section looks at the ongoing problem of amoral, ethical and unethical leadership with case studies and examples and multiple perspectives. The second section examines what we mean ethical and wise leader behavior. The final section examines ethical and wise leadership, with suggestions on actions we can take at the organizational and individual level in dealing with amoral, immoral and unethical leaders, and how to develop further a culture of integrity, ethics and morality.

CHAPTER 1

The Decline of Moral, Ethical and Wise Leaders

"Divorced from ethics, leadership is reduced to management and politics to mere technique"

— *James Macgregor Burns*

There is a long history of corrupt, amoral and unethical business and political leaders in America that go all the way back to the country's creation.

In recent times, we are all familiar with famous fraud cases of Enron, WorldCom, and Tyco. Add to those the following:

- Bernie Madoff, once chairman of NASDAQ, convicted and jailed for a massive illegal investment scheme.

- Joseph Nacchio, former CEO of Qwest, convicted for illegally inflating revenue, illegal trading and fraud regarding financial documents submitted to the Federal Government.

- Walter Forces, CEO of Cendant, convicted of fraud.

- Richard Scrushy, CEO of HealthSouth, convicted of illegal accounting practices, securities fraud and money laundering.

- John Rigas, CEO of Adelphia, convicted of securities, bank and wire fraud.

- Sanjay Kumar, CEO of Computer Associates, convicted of securities fraud.

- Elizabeth Anne Holmes, CEO of Theranos, charged with fraud and named by Fortune as one of the "World's Most Disappointing Leaders."

- Wells Fargo Bank, convicted for opening 1.5 million fraudulent deposit accounts and illegally charging customers fees and fined $ 3 billion.

- And, after the 2008 financial crisis, AIG had no problem doling out millions in bonuses to the very people who drove the company and the country into a financial crisis.

- Charles Kushner, the wealthy New Jersey developer and father of Donald Trump's son-in-law Jared Kushner, was convicted and served a prison sentence for tax fraud and making illegal campaign donations that grew into a bizarre tale involving sex tapes and a prostitute.

- An example of how leaders with low ethical standards can facilitate moral disengagement comes from the trial of Kweku Adoboli, the rogue trader from UBS ultimately sentenced to 7 years in prison for illegal activity that cost the bank $2.3 billion. After earning $6 million on a trade that exceeded his daily limit by $100 million, his supervisor congratulated rather than penalized him.

- And then there is the Enron massive fraud committed by several executives. Kenneth L. Lay, the former chairman and chief executive of Enron was convicted of fraud and conspiracy. Jeffrey Skilling, the Chief Executive Officer, developed a staff of executives that, by the use of accounting loopholes, special purpose entities, and poor financial reporting, were able to hide billions of dollars in debt from failed deals and projects. He was later convicted of fraud and conspiracy charges. Andrew Fastow, the Chief Financial Officer of Enron, was charged with securities fraud, wire fraud, mail fraud, money laundering and conspiracy. Paula Rieker, the Enron vice president responsible for investor relations, pleaded guilty to insider trading. Enron executive Michael Kopper would go on to plead guilty to conspiracy to commit wire fraud and money laundering conspiracy.

- Lehman Brothers prior to the 2008 was the largest trader on the London Stock Exchange and the fourth largest on the New York Stock Exchange. Lehman's 2008 collapse—with record debts of $613 billion— substantially eclipsed both Enron and WorldCom, making it the largest bankruptcy in U.S. corporate history. Researchers have identified Richard Fuld,

CEO of Lehman is the prime cause of that collapse. He displayed many of the characteristics of a corporate psychopath.

Unethical behavior that can be defined as "actions that are intended to promote the effective functioning of the organization or its members (e.g., leaders) and violate core societal values, norms, laws, or standards of proper conduct to exaggerate the truth about one's company's products or services to customers and clients to benefit one's company." Such behavior appears to help the organization in the short term, but comes at a high cost to the business in the long run.

For example, Kobe Steel admitted to falsification over past years relating to large quantities of some types of material, with its employees (including managers) in multiple outlets forging data for the economic benefit of the company. This scandal has gone on to have a huge negative impact on both the company and the wider Japanese steel industry.

The most recent story to add to this partial list is the blatant corruption in the Trump administration where the President and many of his appointees and followers have been charged with and/or convicted of crimes.

As a former CEO, executive coach and leadership trainer for the past 35 years, I have been alarmed by two parallel developments which I believe are actually connected:

1. The prevalence of amoral and unethical senior leaders in institutions and organizations.

2. The lack (and sometimes total absence of) leader wisdom in decision-making, which translates into pervasive policies and practices that harm people and the environment.

The combination of these two phenomena has had disastrous results on the well-being of people and this planet. It emphasizes the dire need to recruit, train and promote wise, moral and ethical leaders. It seems that no matter where we look today, the erosion of ethics and basic moral principles of right and wrong have taken us to the point where trust in our institutions and the very systems that make our society work are in imminent danger.

Celia Moore and her colleagues published a study centering on the role of "Leaders Matter Morally: The Role of Ethical Leadership in Shaping Employee Moral Cognition and Misconduct," in the *Journal of Applied Psychology*, which found that leaders with low-ethical standards amplify their subordinates' tendencies to morally disengage. For instance, Moore contends, if one has a leader who defines success in terms of results rather than the means through which they are obtained, subordinates could more easily morally justify short-changing customers in the interest of profit (and the greater good of company performance).

Leaders who demand obedience or absolute loyalty from their subordinates facilitate their subordinates' displacement of responsibility, such that individual employees can shift their moral agency onto their domineering leader. A leader who refers to clients or competition as a resource to be exploited or an enemy to be overcome can support euphemistic labeling of harmful practices or the attribution of blame for mistreatment onto those whom they are harming. Similarly, a leader's exclusive focus on profits, emphasizing meeting targets, goals, and operational efficiencies can create a situation in which unethical behavior has no apparent victim.

According to other research studies, leaders are considered unethical if they frequently operate with an egotistic intent, utilize controlling as opposed to empowering strategies to influence followers, and fail to abstain from vices. Additionally, leaders are typically regarded as unethical if their actions are grounded in manipulation and exploitation.

Leader behaviors that can be considered unethical include falsifying information, provoking distrust among others, blaming followers for their own mistakes, and showing favoritism in exchange for self-serving actions. In distinguishing ethical from unethical charismatic leaders, researchers noted that unethical leaders use power for personal gain; promote their own personal vision; censure opposing views; demand their own decisions be accepted without question; engage in one-way communication; show insensitivity to followers' needs; and rely on convenient external moral standards to satisfy self-interests.

CHAPTER 2

Corruption and the Unethical Behavior of Leaders, and Organizations

"Wherever there is power, greed, and money, there is corruption."

— Ken Poirot

E ven before the pandemic, an estimated $455 billion of the $7.35 trillion spent annually on healthcare worldwide was lost to fraud and corruption. Today, as governments are ramping up pandemic response spending to unprecedented levels with understandable urgency and desperation, the risk of corruption and misappropriation has increased exponentially.

A recent survey by a German anti-fraud consulting company found that a majority of the 58 countries surveyed experienced corruption related to purchasing and/or access to personal protective equipment during the COVID-19 virus pandemic. And a report from the Lawyers Council for Civil and Economic Rights found that government contracts for the coronavirus response have been riddled with irregularities in dozens of countries.

Corruption is not restricted to Third World countries. Between 1990 and 2002, US federal prosecutors convicted more than 10,000 government officials of acts of official corruption, such as conflict of interest, fraud, campaign-finance violations, and obstruction of justice. The governors of both New Jersey and Connecticut have had to resign amidst allegations of corrupt practices. The past three insurance commissioners of Louisiana have been convicted for official misdeeds.

Transparency International, a non-profit institution annually ranking countries according the prevalence of corruption each country, has released the 2020 Corruption Index.

2020 Corruption Index by Transparency International:

Country Rank (The higher the score, the less corrupt)

Denmark	1	88
New Zealand	2	87
Sweden	3	85
Singapore	3	85
Finland	3	85
Norway	6	84
Netherlands	7	82
Canada	8	81
Luxemburg	9	81
Germany	10	80
United Kingdom	11	80
Australia	12	79
Austria	13	78

Hong Kong	14	76
Iceland	15	73
Belgium	16	73
Japan	17	73
Ireland	18	73
Estonia	19	73
France	20	72
United States	21	71

In addition, The World Economic Forum's "The Global Competitiveness Report on Corruption" shows corruption to be a rather pervasive problem in the U.S., compared to most other OECD countries (the higher the number # the more corrupt):

- On "Diversion of Public Funds [due to corruption]," the U.S. ranks #34.

- On "Irregular Payments and Bribes" (which is perhaps an even better measure of lack of corruption) the U.S. is #42.

- On "Public Trust in Politicians," the U.S. is #54.

- On "Judicial Independence," the U.S. is #38.

- On "Favoritism in Decisions of Government Officials" (otherwise known as governmental "cronyism"), the U.S. is #59.

- On "Organized Crime," the U.S. is #87.

- On "Ethical Behavior of Firms," the U.S. is #29.

- On "Transparency of Governmental Policymaking," the U.S. is #56.

- On "Property Rights" protection (the basic law-and-order measure), the U.S. is #42.

Unethical behavior has entered the White House on several occasions with Presidents James Buchanan, Andrew Jackson, Warren G. Harding, Andrew Johnson, Richard Nixon, and many would argue, Donald Trump.

During his presidency Trump blatantly ignored the emoluments clause of the Constitution, handed taxpayers a multimillion-dollar bill for his frequent trips to his own properties, appointed his daughter and son-in-law to sensitive positions for which they are manifestly unqualified; been impeached twice by Congress for the abuse of power and incitement of insurrection; offered Presidential pardons in return for some future financial favors; and surrounded himself with a host of people who have either been investigated for or convicted of crimes.

"Integrity, transparency and the fight against corruption have to be part of our culture. They have to be thought of as fundamental values."

— Angel Gurria, OECD Secretary General

But the recent problems of unethical behavior predated Trump and his entourage. Consider:

- **The 2008 Financial Crisis.** To some extent, the 2008 financial crisis is a case study of hubris, where self-styled "masters of the universe" convinced themselves that they had devised financial instruments that had reduced the risk of a panic to miniscule levels. But the crisis also exposed systemic corruption inside key financial institutions. It wasn't just a few crooked mortgage brokers offering many bad loans; it also involved serious abuses by ratings agencies, investment banks, government-backed lenders like Fannie Mae, and even some academic economists.

- **The Boeing 737 Max.** The more we learn about the second crash of a Boeing 737 Max aircraft, the more disturbing the tale becomes. While a final determination of the causes of the two recent crashes has yet to be made, it seems increasingly clear that Boeing rushed the new plane to market, downplayed the need for additional pilot training, and used an increasingly cozy relationship with Federal Aviation Administration regulators to win approval for the plane. The world seems to have awakened to the conflicts of interest here: The United States was the last country to ground the plane after the second crash, and Ethiopian authorities chose to send the black boxes for analysis to France rather than to the United States.

- **The College Admissions Scandal.** It's no secret that admission to elite institutions of higher education isn't the pure meritocracy that universities attempt to convey. Being part of an alumni family (a "legacy") is a big plus, and it seems to help a lot if a parent gives the university a large donation at just the right time.

11

But the revelations that wealthy parents and celebrities were colluding with William Singer (a professional "admissions counselor") and a bunch of corrupt coaches and administrators to get their less-than-fully-qualified kids into elite schools by falsifying test results or passing them off as gifted athletes was still an eye-opener. It was also more evidence—as if any were needed—of the corrupting role professional sports play in the life of American universities.

Amoral, Immoral and Unethical Leader Behavior

- Venerated institutions in American life—including the military and the clergy—have been rocked by serious scandals over the past several decades. In addition to the horrifying history of sexual predation and cover-ups in the Catholic Church, the U.S. military has been wrestling with a serious problem of sexual assault in the ranks. A prominent wide-spread procurement scandal rocked the U.S. Navy, and in 2014 thirty-four missile launch control officers conspired to falsify scores on proficiency exams.

- Former Republican Speaker of the House **Dennis Hastert** was indicted on federal charges of structuring bank withdrawals after prosecutors alleged Hastert had molested at least four boys as young as 14 and attempted to compensate his victims and subsequently conceal the transactions. Hastert eventually admitted that he sexually abused the boys whom he had coached

12

decades earlier, and was sentenced to fifteen months in prison.

- **Republican Tim Nolan**, chairman of Donald Trump's presidential campaign in Kentucky, pleaded guilty to child sex trafficking and on February 11, 2018 he was sentenced to serve 20 years in prison.

- Republican state Senator **Ralph Shortey** was indicted on four counts of human trafficking and child pornography. In November 2017, he pleaded guilty to one count of child sex trafficking in exchange for the dropping of the other charges.

- Republican judge **Mark Pazuhanich** pleaded no contest to fondling a 10-year old girl and was sentenced to 10 years' probation.

- Democratic New York Congressman, **Anthony Weiner,** pleaded guilty to transferring obscene material to a minor as part of a plea agreement for sexting and sending Twitter DMs to underage girls as young as 15.

- Democratic Mayor of Racine, Wisconsin, **Gary Becker,** was convicted of attempted child seduction, child pornography, and other child sex crimes.

- Democratic Seattle Mayor **Ed Murray** resigned after multiple accusations of child sexual abuse were levied against him including by family members.

Research has shown that for decades the main reason chief executives were ousted from their jobs was poor financial performance of the firm. In 2018, that changed. Personal misconduct occurring in the #MeToo era is now the biggest driver behind a chief executive falling from the top.

That's according to a new study from the consulting division of PwC, one the nation's largest auditing firms. It is the first time since the group began tracking executive turnover 19 years ago that scandals over bad behavior rather than poor financial performance were the leading cause of leadership dismissals among the world's 2,500 largest public companies.

"A lot of bad actors are being cleared out of the reaches of corporate America," John Paul Rollert, a professor at the University of Chicago who studies the ethics of leadership, told NPR.

Thirty-nine percent of the 89 CEOs who departed in 2018 left for reasons related to unethical behavior stemming from allegations of sexual misconduct or ethical lapses connected to things like fraud, bribery and insider trading, the study found.

Poor financial performance of firms as the reason why CEOs were terminated occurs only about 25% of the time. And that shift, the researchers say, is meaningful. Increasingly, according to the study, corporate boards are approaching allegations of executive misconduct with a "zero-tolerance stance," fueled in part by societal pressures since the rise of the #MeToo movement.

"For companies, they are recognizing that if they don't get aggressive with this type of behavior, they are going to face exceptional liabilities when it comes to court cases," Rollert said. "And so better to address these concerns now than to deal with multi-million-dollar lawsuit and the bad PR that comes with that sometime down the road."

Some former CEOs say the study is proof that more women are feeling emboldened to share stories of alleged abuse or misconduct, and it is reshaping corporate America.

"Employees are starting to say, 'how can you enforce a policy on us without holding CEOs accountable?' " said Bill George, a senior fellow at Harvard Business School and former chief executive of Medtronic, who has served on the boards of Goldman Sachs and Exxon Mobil. "The CEO's behavior has to be beyond reproach. Boards are aware of this and are really feeling pressure around that now," George explained.

The Contagion of Unethical Organizational Behavior

A study by He Bin and Sun Xu published in the *Frontiers of Psychology* concluded "Unethical pro-organizational behavior" (UPB) can now be defined as 'actions that are intended to promote the effective functioning of the organization or its members (e.g., leaders) and violate core societal values, norms, laws, or standards of proper conduct', such as a tendency to exaggerate the truth about one's company's products or services to customers and clients to benefit one's company."

15

Such behavior appears to help the organization in the short term, the researchers argue, but it comes at a high cost to the business in the long run. For example, Kobe Steel has admitted to falsification over past years relating to large quantities of some types of material, with its employees (including managers) in multiple outlets forging data for the economic benefit of the company. This scandal has gone on to have a huge impact on both the company and the wider Japanese steel industry.

Furthermore, He Bin and Sun Xu argue, organizations often develop norms that tolerate the violation of moral standards if it is beneficial to the organization. Studies have shown that, when people are surrounded by the unethical behavior of their peers, they are likely to imitate the behavior of these peers, because such behaviors demonstrate apparently appropriate organizational norms. Therefore, when observing UPB, subordinates will likely consider such behavior to be what the organization expects them to do, and they may then follow and engage in UPB themselves.

How Power Facilitates Unethical Behavior

As the saying goes, with great power comes great responsibility — and yet it seems like so many powerful people use their power for evil, not good. But a new study suggests that tweaking how powerful people think about their power could affect how they act.

Simply put, researcher Miao Hu contends in his study published in the journal *Personality and Social Psychology*

Bulletin, "making people in power think about how they should act (as opposed to how powerful people generally do act) may help them act more ethically". In the study, researchers asked participants to describe how people in power act and also to describe how people in power should be expected to act.

Hu, an assistant professor of marketing at the University of Hawaii at Manoa and the lead author on the study, found that when people were in the position of power and were asked to think about how they would act, they were more ethical. That is, they were more likely to lie about their behavior than were those who were not in a position of power. When the people in the position of power were asked to think about how they should act, on the other hand, they acted more ethically.

"Making people in power think about how they should behave may serve as a potential form of preventative medicine against the abuse of power."

—Miao Hu

How the Media Has Fuelled Unethical Leader Behavior

Stephen Chen, writing in the *Journal of Public Affairs*, says misreporting of a firm's financial performance increases the CEO's confidence which in turn increases the need to misreport performance in order to feed an ever increasing ego. This growth can be fuelled by statements by third party financial analysts and the press which praise their actions. And the actions are not restricted to financial data.

These ethical issues include women exploitation, subliminal perception, and advertising to children, and deceptive advertising. The fact that potentially unethical advertisements are reaching the marketplace suggested that current methods of evaluating advertisements may be insufficient for some of today's controversial or innovative campaigns.

In its more corrosive application — the one that is inculcated in many business schools, and enforced by corporate lawyers and demanded by activist investors and Wall Street analysts — maximizing shareholder value has meant doing whatever is necessary to boost the share price this quarter and the next. Over the years, an exclusive focus on shareholder value has been used to justify cheating or deceiving customers, squeezing workers and suppliers, avoiding taxes and lavishing stock options on executives. Most of what people find so distasteful about American capitalism — the ruthlessness, the greed, the inequality — has its roots in this misguided and twisted notion that business only exists for financial gain for the shareholders (and greedy CEOs).

In an article entitled "Bolstering unethical leaders: The role of the media, financial analysts and shareholders," in the *Journal of Public Affairs*, researcher Stephen Chen describes cites several high profile accounting scandals such as Enron, WorldCom. Chen asserts that the problems resulting from financial incentives and CEO narcissism are accentuated by reports by external parties such as financial analysts and the financial press because increasingly many CEOs are now assessed on the achievement of earnings targets set by financial analysts and investors.

The Impact of Unethical Business and Political Practices

According to a 2006 *Business for Social Responsibility* brief, "Corruption and Bribery", an organization has many reasons for operating ethically, including avoiding fines and litigation, reducing damage to the firm's reputation, protecting or increasing capital and shareholder value, direct and indirect cost control, creating a competitive advantage, and avoiding internal corruption.

On the other hand, unethical behavior in firms results in lower productivity, especially among highly skilled employees, according to "The Relationship of Ability and Satisfaction to Job Performance", in the *Journal of Cross Cultural Psychology,* by Philip E. Varca and Marsha James-Valutis.

Unethical behavior also results in lower long-term financial performance as measured by metrics such as economic value-added, and market value-added as shown in the 2003 study "Does Business Ethics Pay?" in the *Institute of Business Ethics,* by Simon Webley and Elise More.

All of these are documented results of unethical business behavior according to "The Wealth Effects of Unethical Business Behavior," in the *Journal of Economics and Finance,* by Michael D. Long and Spuma Rao.

Edson Spencer, former chairman of Honeywell, in his article "The Hidden Costs of Organizational Dishonesty" in the *Sloan Management Review*, argues it takes years to build a reputation for integrity that can be lost overnight.

And once an organization loses its reputation for integrity, the effect can be permanent, according to the 2004 Josephson Institute report, "The Hidden Costs of Unethical Behavior."

As senior executive unethical behaviors flourish, workers throughout the organization note them, almost as permission to replicate, and unethical behavior becomes a cultural norm. Ultimately, this culture results in detrimental behaviors such as under delivering on promises, turf-guarding, goal-lowering, budget-twisting, fact-hiding, detail-skipping, credit-hogging, and scapegoating, according to studies conducted by the Online Center for Engineering and Science at Case Western Reserve University.

The U.S. Ethics and Compliance Initiative, (ECI) the oldest nonprofit in the ethics & compliance industry is a research and membership organization comprised by institutions across every sector, each dedicated to promoting the highest levels of integrity in their operations. ECI has provided some startling data regarding the presence of unethical practices in U.S. organizations.

According to ECI, the single biggest influence on employee conduct is the organization's culture. In strong ethical cultures, wrongdoing is significantly reduced. Yet only one in five employees, according to ECI's study of American business, indicate that their company has such an environment. This status remains largely unchanged over the past decade. Furthermore, in 2017, 40% of employees believed that their company had a weak ethical culture, a trend that has not notably changed since 2000.

In an article in *The New Yorker*, Robin Wright asks the question, "Is America Becoming a Banana Republic?" She says, "the chief principle of 'banana-ism' is that of 'kleptocracy', whereby those in positions of influence use their time in office to maximize their own gains, always ensuring that any shortfall is made up by those unfortunates whose daily life involves earning money rather than making it." She concludes the United States clearly fits those descriptors.

Unethical Behavior Spreads Like a Virus in the Workplace

The National Business Ethics Survey of nearly 4,700 employees at by the Ethics Resource Center (ERC), an independent research firm for the advancement of high ethical standards and practices in public and private organizations, has revealed the percentage of companies with a weak ethical culture is on the rise, as is the number of employees who experienced retaliation for blowing the whistle on observed misconduct. **The report concluded that "American business may be on the cusp of a large downward shift in ethical conduct."**

Among the other conclusions of the report were the following:

21

- The five most frequently observed misconduct events were misuse of company time (33%); abusive behavior (21%); company resource abuse (20%); lying to employees (20%); and violating corporate Internet use policies (16%).

- The proportion of employees who observed misconduct and then decided to report it climbed to a record high of 65%.

- Nearly 70% of workers who witnessed violations involved stealing or improper payment offers to public officials.

- Almost two-thirds of employees reported improper use of competitors' inside information; the falsification of expense reports; trading on inside information; making improper political contributions; delivery of goods or services that failed to meet specifications; abusive behavior or behavior that creates a hostile work environment; and the falsification and/or manipulation of financial reporting information.

- Many of the retaliatory actions were severe: exclusions from decisions and work activity by supervisor or management (64%); verbally abused by supervisor or someone else in management (62%); verbally abused by other employees (51 %); experienced online harassment (31%); experienced physical harm to their person or property (31%); and harassed at home (29%).

- Further, the NBES reported the percentage of employees who perceived pressure to compromise their company's ethical standards, or even break the law so they could perform their jobs, jumped significantly from 13% in 2011 to 29% in 2017.

- As expected, there's a very strong correlation between a strong ethical culture and lower observed misconduct. Misconduct was observed in only 29% of companies with a strong ethical culture but seen in 90% of those with a weak ethical culture.

Celia Moore and her colleagues published an article in the *Journal of Applied Psychology* entitled "Leaders Matter Morally: The Role of Ethical Leadership in Shaping Employee Moral Cognition and Misconduct," and concluded among other things, "leaders with low-ethical standards might amplify their subordinates' propensities to morally disengage."

For instance, Moore states, if one has a leader who defines success in terms of results rather than the means through which they are obtained, subordinates could more easily morally justify short-changing customers in the interest of profit. Moore found that leaders who demand obedience or absolute loyalty from their subordinates facilitate their subordinates' displacement of responsibility, such that individual employees can shift their moral agency onto their domineering leader. A leader who refers to clients or competition as a resource to be exploited or an enemy to be overcome can support euphemistic labeling of harmful practices or the attribution of blame for mistreatment onto those whom they are harming.

Reasons Why We Choose Unethical Leaders

Tomas Chamorro-Premuzic, Chief Talent Scientist at Manpower Group and a Professor of Business Psychology at University College London (UCL) and Columbia University, unpacks the psychology of why we don't choose leaders with the highest integrity.

Here are some of the reasons he cites:

- **We are not serious about integrity.** While we love to say that integrity is a cornerstone of leadership potential, our order of preference, when we vote or appoint leaders, prioritizes other traits. In fact, he says, many of the qualities that seduce us in leaders are diametrically opposed to integrity.

- **We are seduced by narcissistic and psychopathic leaders.** As he shows in his latest book or related TED talk, we have a tendency to gravitate towards charismatic and magnetic personalities, usually big egos, who can captivate us with their megalomaniac visions and delusional talents. Although it is perfectly possible for charismatic leaders to be ethical, when we select leaders on charisma rather than humility, and confidence rather than competence, we should not be surprised that we end up with a lot of unethical and self-centered people in charge, who are quite happy to take advantage of others to advance their own selfish interests.

- **Too many people become leaders to acquire status and power.** Scientists have always regarded leadership as a psychological process of influence whereby an individual enables a group of people to elevate their performance and accomplishments by directing them to function as a cohesive unit. And in politics, leadership brings societies together to propel them to progress and prosperity.

But there is a problem, Chamorro-Premuzic says. Leadership is marketed as the ultimate career destination, and it confers power and status, so there are a great number of individuals who are only interested in becoming leaders to acquire fame and status. They have no desire to make others better and are entirely focused on their own personal success. The more we pretend that leadership is an unselfish and other-oriented role, the more these individuals will fake integrity in order to climb up the ladder.

Chamorro-Premuzic contends: "When leaders emerge to co-opt our own selfish interests, we are quite happy to leave aside higher moral principles, and optimize for our own personal success. This is how a single rotten apple can contaminate the whole barrel, and why good apples go bad when you put them in a rotten barrel. The effects of leadership always cascade down, and corrupt leaders are very good at unleashing their teams' parasitic mindset. In politics, it is often said that most countries have the government they deserve. At least in democracies, we can see why corrupt leaders would be more likely to emerge in societies with corrupt rather than altruistic values."

In an article published in the *Harvard Business Review*, "Overconfidence is Contagious," by Joey T. Cheng, Elizabeth R. Tenney, Don A. Moore and Jennifer M. Logg, they report their detailed research of why the famous American company Enron collapsed. Their search for answers leads consistently to Enron's top executives, Jeffrey Skilling and Kenneth Lay, whose massive acts of accounting fraud, corruption, and deception covered up the company's weaknesses until their exposure led to its downfall.

But a deeper analysis reveals the dysfunctional corporate culture that made it all possible. A "culture of arrogance" permeated the organization, and many employees felt like they were part of an elite group and believed they were smarter than everybody else. This culture of bravado drove employees to aggressively negotiate deals with questionable financials and take on increased risks under the illusion of invincibility. An abundance of research reveals that overconfident leaders put their firms at risk.

Their research shows the havoc these unethical executives create extends beyond their own reckless decision making — they may be the first domino to fall, influencing their employees who in turn influence their peers. Inspiring a culture of overconfidence in this way fuels greater peril.

One lesson, the authors, say, from the story of Enron is that the success of an organization depends on cultivating the right social climate and norms — norms that promote grounding in reality and freedom from delusions of grandeur.

There is research evidence that shows a connection between unethical behavior and a selfishness of rich and powerful people.

The Rich

Social scientists have long known that the rich are not exactly model citizens. They evade taxes more often, flaunt traffic laws that protect pedestrians and donate less frequently to charity. In the aftermath of the Great Recession, there has been no shortage of reports in the popular media on their selfishness and opportunism.

The National Center for Charitable Statistics finds that households earning less than $50,000 donate 4 percent of their adjusted gross income, while those earning $200,000 to $250,000 give away about half that—2.4 percent.

Rich people apparently care less about the less fortunate than their middle-class counterparts.

That's one conclusion drawn from a new study by the *Chronicle of Philanthropy* that found that rich people give a smaller share of their income to charity than middle-class Americans do.

While households that make at least $100,000 per year give an average 4.2 percent of their discretionary income to charity, those that make between $50,000 to $75,000 per year give an average 7.6 percent of their discretionary income to charity, according to the study.

It seems that rich people living in wealthy enclaves are the worst when it comes to thinking of the poor. In ZIP codes where more than 40 percent of taxpayers make more than $200,000 per year, residents give an average 2.8 percent of their discretionary income to charity. Many of those rich residents give no money to charity at all.

The Powerful

Leaders' propensity for generosity seems to depend on whether they feel like they've earned their high-status position, according to new research conducted by psychological scientists Nicholas Hays (Michigan State University) and Steven Blader (New York University).

The findings indicate that a boss or colleague who feels that their high-status position is unearned is likely to be much more generous compared to someone who feels like they're entitled to a spot at the top.

"For instance, high-status CEOs—who have a greater sense of hubris and thus are likely to have an exaggerated sense of their value to their organizations— extract more compensation and yet devote less time and effort to advancing organizational goals compared to lower-status CEO," write Hays and Blader. "Because generosity is often strategically demonstrated to attain status, generosity may decrease once status-attainment goals are achieved."

Previous research published in *Psychological Science* has shown that attaining a position of power really can change people for the worse: Across five experiments, Joris Lammers (Tilburg University) and colleagues found that "irrespective of how power was manipulated or hypocrisy was measured, we found strong evidence that the powerful are more likely to engage in moral hypocrisy than are people who lack power."

However, power only seemed to compromise people's moral judgment under circumstances in which people felt like they had earned their position: "Our final study demonstrated the crucial role of entitlement: Only when power is experienced as legitimate is moral hypocrisy a likely result. If power is not experienced as legitimate, then the moral-hypocrisy effect disappears."

For their first experiment, Hays and Blader surveyed a group of 255 MBA students. The students were working together in 51 teams over the course of a six-month field project with real clients. The students completed two surveys asking them to assess how helpful they were (i.e., "I will be willing to help when needed") and how important they were to their group's success. The first survey was completed at the very beginning of the field project; in a second survey, completed three months into the project, participants also rated each member of their group on a 7-point scale for how much respect, esteem, and prominence they had within their team.

"As predicted, there is a significant positive relationship between status and generosity at low legitimacy and a significant negative relationship at high legitimacy," the researchers report.

A second experiment looked at whether status influenced people's actual behavior. A group of 339 college students were assigned roles in a business scenario, ostensibly based on their scores from a business aptitude assessment. In reality, the participants were randomly assigned to either high- or low-status roles and either legitimacy or illegitimacy conditions.

Those in the legitimate conditions were assigned to a status role that matched their "score" on the assessment, while those in the illegitimate condition were told they'd received a lower score than their team members but would be given a higher-ranking role.

After learning their scores and role assignments, participants played a game in which group members could allocate 100 points among themselves and their two teammates. These points could be exchanged for lottery tickets at the end of the study, and generosity was gauged based on how many points participants allocated to their teammates.

As expected, those who felt they were entitled to a high-status position were significantly less generous towards their teammates than participants who thought their high ranking was not earned. Across all six experiments, those who felt entitled to their high-status position showed significantly less generosity than people who felt they'd ended up at the top through a fluke.

"Complementing previous work indicating that generosity leads to status increases, we find that once an individual has obtained high status, the legitimacy of that status determines whether he or she tends to behave more or less generously than low-status group members," Hays and Blader conclude.

CHAPTER 3

The Narcissistic, Sociopathic and Psychopathic Leader

"Americans are experiencing an epidemic in narcissistic behavior in a culture that is intrinsically self-conscious and selfish, and citizens are encouraged to pursue happiness and instant gratification of their personal desires"

—Kilroy J. Oldster

The "Dark Triad" Personalities

For 15 years, research into dark personality traits (including narcissism has been rapidly expanding. We now know that these traits are far more evident, on average, in men than women. We know that approximately 1-2 per cent of individuals in the general population display extremely dark personality features – enough to meet the clinical threshold for a personality disorder – and about 10-20 per cent of individuals have moderately elevated levels. **We know that even people with moderate levels of dark traits can wreak havoc: They are more likely to lie and cheat, show racist attitudes, and be violent towards others.**

Scott Barry Kaufman reports in his research published in *Scientific American* that in corporate settings, those with dark personality traits are slightly more likely to emerge as leaders and are seen as charismatic but, when it comes to getting the job done, they tend to achieve less and are considered poor team players.

Kaufman's study also found that political figures with dark personality traits show that they are much poorer at getting legislation passed. Hedge fund managers with these traits generally accrue_significantly lower financial returns on the investment funds they manage. Overall, Kaufman says, individuals with dark traits engage in more counterproductive work behavior, such as theft and abusive supervision. Perhaps unsurprisingly, they don't end up with higher average incomes than their peers with ethical and moral personalities.

Persons who display either narcissistic personality disorder or the narcissistic personality type are preoccupied with maintaining excessively positive self-concepts. They become overly concerned with obtaining positive, aggrandizing feedback from others and react with extreme positive or negative emotions when they succeed or fail to receive confirmation that others hold them in high regard. Narcissists want positive feedback about themselves, and they actively manipulate others to solicit or coerce admiration from them. Accordingly, narcissism is thought to reflect a form of chronic interpersonal self-esteem regulation.

Individuals with a narcissistic personality disorder, according to the American Psychological Association's DSM-5, exhibit five or more of the following, which are present by early adulthood and across contexts:

- A grandiose sense of self-importance.

- Preoccupation with fantasies of unlimited success, power, brilliance, beauty, or ideal love.

- Belief that one is special and can only be understood by or associate with special people or institutions.

- A need for excessive admiration.

- A sense of entitlement (to special treatment).

- Exploitation of others.

- A lack of empathy.

- Envy of others or the belief that one is the object of envy.

- Arrogant, haughty behavior or attitudes.

Individuals with NPD can be easily stung by criticism or defeat and may react with disdain or anger—but social withdrawal or the false appearance of humility may also follow according to the DSM-5.

A sense of entitlement, disregard for other people, and other aspects of NPD can damage relationships. While a person with NPD may be a high-achiever, the personality disorder can also have a negative impact on performance (due to, for instance, one's sensitivity to criticism).

What do Tesla's Elon Musk, Oracle's Larry Ellison, Apple's Steve Jobs, and Lehman Brothers' Dick Fuld have in common? All are or were CEOs who have been associated with outstanding financial success, and some have been linked to catastrophic company failures or brushes with bankruptcy. All of them also have been described at narcissists.

Narcissism is the one personality constellation to which leaders tend to gravitate according to several researchers, so that it is unsurprising to find that a significant number of world leaders have grandiose belief systems and show clear signs of narcissism.

Charles O'Reilly III has studied business narcissists extensively, and says, "We see the 10% of narcissists that succeeded and call them visionaries. We're not looking at the 90% who flamed out and caused irreparable damage."

Narcissistic CEOs Weaken Collaboration and Integrity

In a paper called "When 'Me' Trumps 'We,'" O'Reilly and two researchers from the University of California, Berkeley Haas School of Business, Jennifer Chatman and Bernadette Doerr, examined the kind of company culture that narcissists inspire. Through a series of field tests and surveys, they show that narcissistic managers tend to prefer and create organizational cultures with less collaboration and lower integrity, and that their subordinates are more likely to act accordingly. Past research has shown that narcissists are more likely to seek out leadership positions in the first place — and that they are more likely to lie, cheat, and steal.

"If you deal with a narcissist, it can be unpleasant. If you're married to one, it can be damaging. But fundamentally, individuals can choose to walk away," O'Reilly says. "When narcissists assume positions of power, their effects become hugely magnified."

Understanding the Narcissistic CEO

O'Reilly and his colleagues studied the sort of corporate culture narcissists are likely to cultivate through a series of surveys of over 700 adults through Amazon's Mechanical Turk. In each case, they assessed participants' level of narcissism — often associated with traits like arrogance, self-centeredness, and a lack of empathy — and leadership style. The researchers found that people who were more narcissistic were significantly less likely to value integrity and collaboration. For example, narcissists were less prone to agree with statements such as, "I treat people with care and respect," "I practice what I preach," and "It is important to maintain harmony in the team."

The study's authors also found that more narcissistic people were likelier to support policies and behaviors that reduced collaboration and integrity, such as being willing to look the other way on violations of company policy or promote people who were less ethical. Finally, they concluded that people working for a more narcissistic CEO would make recommendations that reflected less collaboration and integrity, such as being less likely to suggest policies or promotion of candidates who embodied these qualities.

The researchers also surveyed nearly 900 business school alumni from Stanford, Santa Clara University, and UC Berkeley who worked at 56 large, publicly traded high-tech firms based in the United States. Alumni completed surveys to evaluate their CEO's personality type and organizational cultures. Controlling for factors like firm size and length of the CEO's tenure, the researchers found that more narcissistic CEOs were less likely to lead firms with collaborative cultures and an emphasis on integrity.

"Lots of studies show that companies with cultures that are less collaborative and have lower integrity are more likely to get in trouble and violate laws," O'Reilly says. Other studies have shown that narcissistic CEOs are more likely to get bogged down in lengthy litigation and manipulate earnings. O'Reilly and his colleagues are currently designing a study that will explore whether more narcissistic CEOs, as rated by their corporate boards, are more likely to run afoul of the law.

Charismatic Narcissistic Leaders

While charisma is generally considered a highly positive and attractive attribute, it also has negative aspects. Leadership expert Jay Conger points out that there is a "dark side" to charismatic leadership in which untrammeled ambitions and powerful personal forces hold sway.

In general, a leader's vision may project personal need based on underlying neurosis while misreading market demand and availability of resources. For example, Edwin Land of Polaroid sank millions of dollars into the development of his dream camera, priced six times higher than the successful Colorpaks then in high consumer demand. Steve Jobs, An Wang, and John DeLorean also appeared to make major market miscalculations, inducing investors to advance large sums of money for projects that promised to be state-of-the art, but ended up to be expensive failures.

Sometimes, charismatics may destroy a company through wild and unchallenged ambitions that produce an unrealistic vision. Consider, for example, the case of People's Express. The company's charismatic CEO, Donald Burr's expansionism undermined his original success, which was based on no-frills, low-cost service solidified by a tight-knit workforce sharing the profits. After a quick takeoff and supersonic growth, People Express eventually crashed as big competitors undercut Burr's discount fares to prevent him from taking away their customers.

The combination of charisma and narcissism is formidable. Researcher Heinz Kohut notes that narcissistic charismatics "have the uncanny ability to exploit, not necessarily in full awareness, the unconscious feelings of their subordinates." In this process, some followers may try to embrace an "omnipotent" leader, one who will fulfill their dependency needs. In particular, a leader who is both charismatic and narcissistic may be able to make full use of his or her symbolic power to gain follower endorsement of views and actions. Because of his or her narcissism, such a leader may tend toward grandiose visions and bold actions, blaming others when things go wrong. Followers come under the leader's sway and buy into actions and explanations they would ordinarily construe as excessive and self-serving.

Narcissism and CEO Hubris

Researchers Sarosh Asad and Eugene Sadler-Smith have shown in their research the connection between hubris and narcissism of CEOs. Among their conclusions were:

- They both occupy the darker side of leadership and lead to pernicious effects and potentially destructive outcomes.

- Metaphorically, "hubrists" are intoxicated with positional power and prior success, but for narcissists, power facilitates self-intoxication.

- Hubris is a grandiose sense of self, characterized by disrespectful attitudes toward others and a misperception of one's place in the world.

- Researchers have pointed out how many of today's leaders epitomize narcissism in their personalities and are hubristic regarding their leadership behaviors that society appears to be becoming more narcissistic and that there appears to be a hubris 'epidemic' among leaders.

- Many recent and notorious corporate scandals were precipitated by CEOs who exhibited hubris and/or narcissism (e.g. Elizabeth Holmes at Theranos, Martin Winterkorn at Volkswagen, Kenneth Lay and Jeffrey Skilling at Enron, Calisto Tanzi at Parmalat, Dick Fuld at Lehman Brothers, Jan Carlzon at SAS Airlines, and Carlos Ghosn at Nissan.) Such scandals sparked intense interest in and concern for how these attributes among leaders could be among the antecedents of corporate fraud, environmental degradations, various destructive leadership unethical practices.

- Quintessentially, hubristic leaders become intoxicated with power and prior successes, and thus they become overconfident in their abilities, overestimate the probability of further successful outcomes, simultaneously underestimate what can go wrong, are contemptuous toward and disparage the advice and criticism of others, and create conditions that invite or give rise to negative unintended consequences.

A research report by MWM Consulting on the risk of narcissistic, arrogant and power-hungry behavior by CEOs, "Taming Narcissus", suggests that the unchecked personalities of senior leaders can become a major destructive force and harder to detect than other corporate threats.

For MWM's study, more than 80 CEOs, chairmen and board directors shared their experience (successful and unsuccessful) of identifying high-risk CEOs across 400 boards in 21 countries. Michael Reyner, managing partner at MWM, says: "If their behavior becomes distorted and is unchecked, a once enormously positive and talented CEO can begin to imperil the business. If the CEO stops listening to advice and there are not sufficient checks and balances, the business can make flawed decisions. Equally, the culture can become corrupted with people unable to be open and say what they think, believing that they have to ingratiate themselves with the CEO."

In his book, *Why Do So Many Incompetent Men Become Leaders (and how to fix it),* psychologist Tomas Chamorrow-Premuzic argues convincingly, "although men make up a majority of leaders, they underperform when compared with female leaders. In fact, most organizations equate leadership potential with a handful of destructive personality traits, like overconfidence and narcissism…. The result is a deeply flawed system that rewards arrogance rather than humility and loudness rather than wisdom."

In my article, "Our Obsession with Narcissistic Leaders When Humble Leaders Are Better," in *The Financial Post,* I argue, "The public in general and even management experts are hypocritical about what makes a good leader. On the one hand we exalt and praise leaders who are basically nasty and abusive (called assholes by some) because they are financially successful and on the other hand, research shows that humble leaders whose focus is to serve others are equally successful, but more importantly, capture the hearts and loyalty of others. Which do we value more?"

There is a dark downside to this appearance of success Charles O'Reilly contends. Company morale often declines, and employees leave the company. And while the narcissistic or abusive leaders may bring in the bigger paychecks, O'Reilly says there is compelling evidence that they don't perform any better than lower-paid, less narcissistic counterparts. This argument has been supported by Michael Maccoby in his book, *The Productive Narcissist: The Promise and Peril of Visionary Leadership.*

Robert Sutton was one of the first leadership experts to draw attention to the prevalence of abusive bosses and how organizations should screen them out, as detailed in his book, *The No Asshole Rule: Building a Civilized Workplace and Surviving One That Isn't.* He points out that tech firms, particularly those in Silicon Valley are where abusive leaders thrive.

He says in business and sports it is assumed if you are a big winner, you can get away with being an asshole. Sutton argues such bosses and cultures drive good people out and claims bad bosses affect the bottom line through increased turnover, absenteeism, decreased commitment and performance. He says the time spent counselling or appeasing these people, consoling victimized employees, reorganizing departments or teams and arranging transfers produce significant hidden costs for the company. And he warns organizations this behavior is contagious.

The Current Business Model and Narcissists

Steve Jobs has been called the greatest businessman the world has ever seen and the best CEO of this generation. But he's also the same man who would yell at people for 30 minutes straight; cut in front of his employees at lunch time; berate hospitality and restaurant staff; park in handicapped spaces; call HR personnel people with "mediocre mentality;" and told his staff how much they "sucked."

Walter Isaacson's biography *Steve Jobs* didn't just create a Hollywood hit: It created a manual for any bosses seeking a hall pass for their temper tantrums. In other words, it's okay to tell your employees that their work is shit and to park your Mercedes across two handicapped parking spaces—as long as the end result is a financially successful product.

Somewhere along the way, it seems that Silicon Valley decided that internet connectivity matters more than human connectivity; that a surfeit of technical intelligence can make up for a dearth of emotional intelligence. After all, if it worked for a genius like Jobs, it can't be that bad.

For instance, Mark Zuckerberg, one of the richest men in the world, famously ousted his friend Eduardo Saverin from Facebook. He also stole his business idea from the Winklevoss twins. "Yah, I'm going to fuck them," he told a friend over IM about the pair. "Probably in the ear."

Snapchat CEO Evan Spiegel wrote a number of misogynistic-sounding emails when he was in college to his fraternity brothers. Once, Spiegel was so angry with his parents, he reportedly cut himself out of family photos.

Twitter's co-founders back-stabbed each other repeatedly: Founder Noah Glass was booted out of the company. Ev Williams and Jack Dorsey were both given, and then stripped of, the CEO title because of their abusive behavior.

Mark Suster, a prominent Los Angeles-based investor, isn't sure what to make of assholes in business. He lists "integrity" as a bonus characteristic when it comes to top entrepreneurs' DNA. "I believe that integrity and honesty are very important to most venture capital investors," he wrote on his blog, *Both Sides of the Table,* "unfortunately, I don't believe that they are required to make a lot of money."

Tom McNichol wrote in the *Atlantic:* "CEOs, middle managers and wannabe masters of the universe are currently devouring the Steve Jobs biography and thinking to themselves: 'See! Steve Jobs was an asshole and he was one of the most successful businessmen on the planet. Maybe if I become an even bigger asshole I'll be successful like Steve.'"

A University of Iowa study, *"Perpetuating Abusive Supervision: Third-Party Reactions to Abuse in the Workplace",* found "when a supervisor's performance outcomes are high, abusive behavior tends to be overlooked when they evaluate that supervisor's effectiveness." In other words, while people might not want to be friends with an abusive, overbearing bosses, they'll tolerate their behavior as long as they are productive.

All the media attention that's given to Jobs and his legacy, as well as political figures like Donald Trump, leads us to believe that *all* successful leaders are charismatic. But if we broadened the spotlight to include every manager on earth, we'd see that charisma is generally a poor predictor of successful leadership.

In fact, charisma is sometimes merely a cover for "dark" personality traits like narcissism, because narcissists are especially skilled at managing the impression they make on other people. Chamorro-Premuzic estimates that between 20% and 30% of charismatic leaders are also narcissists.

So it seems that abusive, narcissistic bosses are alive and doing well in the business world (and politics), and even exalted by the media.

Theo Veldsman of the University of Johannesburg has published a study on the growth and impact of toxic leadership on organizations. He contends that "there is a growing incidence of toxic leadership in organizations across the world." Veldsman says that anecdotal and research evidence shows that one out of every five leaders is toxic, and he argues according to his research, that is closer to three out of every ten leaders.

Veldsman describes toxic leadership as "ongoing, deliberate intentional actions by a leader to undermine the sense of dignity, self-worth and efficacy of an individual. This results in exploitative, destructive, devaluing and demeaning work experiences." He goes on to say that a toxic organization is one that "erodes, disables and destroys the physiological, psychosocial and spiritual well being of the people who work in it in permanent and deliberate way."

Paul Babiak's book *Snakes in Suits* profiles how some functional psychopaths can fake it until they make it up the corporate ladder through charm and guile, pointing out how statistically significant evidence shows psychopaths are overrepresented in corporate America.

Researchers at Pennsylvania State University found that the firms with narcissistic CEOs did not perform any better than the firms with non-narcissistic CEOs.

Roy Libit, writing in journal the *Academy of Management Executive*, "The long-term organizational impact of destructively narcissistic managers," concluded, "A significant number of managers have a degree of destructive narcissism (DN) in their personalities."

Libit says destructive narcissism particularly limits the ability of managers to work effectively with colleagues and subordinates. Their arrogance, sense of entitlement, lack of concern for others' feelings, devaluation of others' abilities, and desire for the limelight generally seriously compromise their ability to work in teams. Moreover, they not only do a poor job of developing people but alienate subordinates as a result of their devaluation of others, insistence on having their own way, lack of empathy, and willingness to exploit others. "Individuals who continue to work for a DN manager are likely to be promoted; the best people are likely to leave," Libit says.

Furthermore, the good ideas of subordinates are likely to be disparaged lest they draw attention away from the narcissistic manager. Meanwhile, no one dares to criticize the DN manager's ideas, so both creativity and critical assessment of ideas are crippled. In sum, DN managers are markedly compromised in their ability to work with subordinates and peers.

The Corporate Psychopaths and Sociopaths

The Psychopath

"Psychopaths have a grandiose self-structure which demands a scornful and detached devaluation of others, in order to ward off their envy toward the good perceived in other people."

—Robert D. Hare

In my *Financial Post* article, "Why Are There More Psychopaths in the Boardroom?" I said, "When we think about psychopaths, most of us might imagine a Hannibal Lecter or Jeffrey Dahmer. Would we consider that psychopaths might be lurking around boardrooms and CEO corner offices? The reality is quite different. Increasing numbers of corporate psychopaths have brought havoc to the lives of millions of people, economies and entire countries, but executive actually tops the list of jobs with the highest proportion of psychopaths."

"You are 400% more likely to encounter a psychopath in top management than in the NYC subway."

—Dr. Robert Hare, *Snakes in Suits: When Psychopaths*
Go to Work.

While the incidence of psychopathy among the general population is only one percent, some studies show triple or quadruple that percentage of business leaders are psychopaths. Even more alarming research claims that one in five corporate leaders qualifies as having a high level of psychopathic traits." Also, "The desire for power, status, and money characterizing dark triad individuals may steer them toward, for example, economics, business, and law educations because these educations pave the way for a career in the corporate world, and the corporate world generally rewards self-serving behavior and provides an environment in which individuals with dark personalities can make use of their qualities and succeed," commented the researchers.

Research conducted by forensic psychologist Nathan Brooks from Bond University found 21 per cent of 261 corporate professionals he studied had clinically significant psychopathic traits.

Researchers Henry S. Cheang and Steven H. Appelbaum studied corporate psychopathy and toxic leaders and identified the following features of corporate psychopaths: "manipulativeness," extreme dishonesty, grandiosity, lack of empathy, lack of emotion, lack of remorse and failure to accept responsibility.

49

The hallmarks of the psychopathic personality involve egocentric, grandiose behavior, completely lacking empathy and a conscience. Additionally, psychopaths may be charismatic, charming, and adept at manipulating one-on-one interactions. In a corporation, one's ability to advance is determined in large measure by a person's ability to favorably impress the boss. Unfortunately, certain of these psychopathic qualities – in particular charm, charisma, grandiosity (which can be mistaken for vision or confidence) and the ability to "perform" convincingly in one-on-one settings – are also qualities that can help one get ahead in the business world.

Clive Body has published a number of studies describing the characteristics and behaviors of psychopathic corporate leaders. Corporate psychopaths' behavior was marked by high levels of abusive control. The corporate psychopaths were seen as being organizational stars and as deserving of awards by those above them, while they simultaneously subjected those below them to extreme behavior, including bullying, intimidation and coercion. The corporate psychopaths also engaged in extreme forms of mismanagement characterized by poor personnel management, directionless leadership, mismanagement of resources and fraud.

With their conscience-free approach to life and willingness to lie to present themselves in the best possible light, corporate psychopaths are, to some extent, products of modern business. In particular, the increasing pace of business and fast turnover of personnel combined with the relatively shallow appointment procedures, which do not uncover their personality flaws, has allowed them to advance.

Furthermore, Western-style business has promoted psychopathic managers because of their ruthless willingness to "get the job done". However, as they attain senior positions, corporate psychopaths have become architects of ruthlessness as they create a culture of extremes. Their characteristics of being ultra-rational, financially oriented managers with no emotional concern for or empathy with other employees, marks them as apparently useful to the style of capitalism.

Corporate psychopaths have also been reported to constitute the largest threat to business ethics across the world. Financial insiders as well as psychologists and management researchers agree that corporate psychopaths within banks were linked to the global financial crisis of 2008. These ideas have been supported by research which finds that psychopathy scores are higher among finance students than they are among other students.

In a 2019 study, published in the journal *Academy of Management*, scientists asked the question: What if leaders in organizations are guided by the wrong values, lack a moral compass and compassion for others, and use their positions to pursue their own goals?

The research highlights the power of individual "bad actors" at work, whose behavior can "toxify" a company. The study also reveals how one can spot a "dark triad" behavior among their coworkers: What, exactly, should you do if your coworker is acting like a psychopath, narcissist, or Machiavellian?

Two psychology researchers, Delroy Paulhus and Kevin M. Williams, coined the term "dark triad" in 2002, a constellation of three socially aversive, partly overlapping traits: narcissism, Machiavellianism, and psychopathy, the study's authors describe. All three traits are characterized by the "tendency to influence others for selfish gains."

Generally, the dark triad involves people who show some of these red flag behaviors but not necessarily enough to be diagnosed with narcissistic or antisocial personality disorders in a clinical setting.

Machiavellians always look out for themselves. Machiavellians are sly, deceptive, distrusting, and manipulative, researchers say. They also tend to be cynical, dislike humanity, and are callous, striving for goals like money, power, and status.

While Machiavellians don't have to be the star of the show, they tend to be highly strategic, acting like a puppeteer pulling strings behind the curtain. At work, Machiavellians sometimes hide knowledge from others as a way to get ahead. They will also consider lying, cheating, and misrepresenting information if that helps them to control a situation. Meanwhile, they are good at forming political alliances and cultivating a charismatic image if it benefits their personal agenda.

"There is the possibility that the behavior of dark triad followers can have a contagious effect on team members, meaning that other team members might mimic or copy the negative strategic behaviors of dark triad followers," the study authors write.

Often, the negative behaviors of one person can reduce trust, elicit negative feelings, and lead to perceptions of inequity. In turn, team members can become defensive, have angry outbursts, or withdraw. These downstream effects ultimately hamper cooperation, creativity, and performance.

Clearly then there are commonalities and overlaps between these psychopathic, narcissistic and Machiavellian personalities and they are all relatively dark personalities compared to normal people.

Government and Financial sectors have the highest numbers of Corporate Psychopaths in them, as is shown in research. This would lead to the expectation that these sectors would score the lowest on measures of corporate social responsibility. This is indeed mainly the case.

The Sociopath

In the business world, 4% of the population exhibits sociopathic tendencies. They thrive in organizational settings where money and status enter the equation, and often work their way up to positions of power.

Sociopathy is not a clinical term, meaning it is not endorsed by the American Psychiatric Association, nor is it used by most mental health professionals. The clinical terms that capture sociopathic behavior are either psychopathy or Anti-Social Personality Disorder.

Sociopathy refers to a pattern of antisocial behaviors and attitudes, including manipulation, deceit, aggression, and a lack of empathy for others. Sociopaths may or may not break the law, but by exploiting and manipulating others, they violate the trust that the human enterprise runs on.

The defining characteristic of the sociopath is a profound lack of conscience—a flaw in the moral compass that typically steers people away from breaking common rules and toward treating others decently. This disconnect, however, may be hidden by a charming demeanor.

A psychopath doesn't have a conscience. If he lies to you so he can steal your money, he won't feel any moral qualms, though he may pretend to. He may observe others and then act the way they do so he's not "found out," Most sociopaths have a tendency to require positive attention and reinforcement from others; a corporate environment is the perfect place for these skills to blossom and develop, all at the expense of others.

Both lack empathy, the ability to stand in someone else's shoes and understand how they feel. But a psychopath has less regard for others, says Aaron Kipnis, PhD, author of *The Midas Complex*. Someone with this personality type sees others as objects he can use for his own benefit.

Here's an official description of what a sociopath is, but from an organizational perspective, the behaviors below suggest how to spot a sociopath in business. To gauge if you're working with one, ask yourself if the person in question:

- Superficially compliments an individual and then quickly attacks and/or criticizes them in much greater depth?

- Displays a sense of superiority and talks down to others?

- Addresses and subsequently changes topics in an apparently random fashion?

- Displays a micro-focus on topics of intense interest to them which don't relate to significant (or even real) organizational issues?

- Repeatedly undermines progress by creating havoc and disruption within the organization?

- Appears to live in a "fictional world" where their intentions, behaviors, and actions appear to have little relationship to reality?

- Accuses others of the very detrimental behaviors they display?

- Is tremendously contradictory in their behavior without any apparent rhyme or reason for their actions?

- Spreads falsehoods for no obvious reason, including lies which don't seem to even directly benefit them?

- Alternates between showing another person intense focus and then completely ignoring them?

CHAPTER 4

What is Moral and Ethical?

*"Whoever is careless with the truth in small matters
cannot be trusted with important matters."*

—Albert Einstein

A distinction must be made between the terms "amoral" and "immoral." Amoral can be defined as not involving questions of right or wrong; without moral quality; neither moral nor immoral; having no moral standards, restraints, or principles; unaware of or indifferent to questions of right or wrong. Immoral can be defined as violating moral principles; not conforming to the patterns of conduct usually accepted or established as consistent with principles of personal and social ethics.

An amoral CEO would not consider whether an action is right or wrong, but rather if it is useful. An immoral CEO would be violating some accepted standard of morality, and would be conscious of his action being wrong.

The word moral derived from a Greek word "Mos" which means custom. On the other hand, if we talk about ethics, it is also derived from a Greek word "Ethikos" which means character. Put simply, morals are the customs established by group of individuals whereas ethics defines the character of an individual.

Generally, the terms *ethics* and *morality* are used interchangeably, although a few different communities (academic, legal, or religious, for example) will occasionally make a distinction. In fact, Britannica's article on ethics considers the terms to be the same as moral philosophy. While understanding that most ethicists (that is, philosophers who study ethics) consider the terms interchangeable, let's go ahead and dive into these distinctions.

Both morality and ethics loosely have to do with distinguishing the difference between "good and bad" or "right and wrong." Many people think of morality as something that's personal and normative, whereas ethics is the standards of "good and bad" defined by a certain community or social setting. For example, your local community may think adultery is immoral, and you personally may agree with that.

However, the distinction can be useful if your local community has no strong feelings about adultery, but you consider adultery immoral on a personal level. By these definitions of the terms, your *morality* would contradict the *ethics* of your community. In popular discourse, however, we'll often use the terms moral and immoral when talking about issues like adultery regardless of whether it's being discussed in a personal or in a community-based situation. As you can see, the distinction can get a bit tricky.

It's important to consider how the two terms have been used in discourse in different fields so that we can consider the connotations of both terms. For example, *morality* has a Christian connotation to many Westerners, since moral theology is prominent in the church. Similarly, *ethics* is the term used in conjunction with business, medicine, or law. In these cases, ethics serves as a personal code of conduct for people working in those fields, and the ethics themselves are often highly debated and contentious. These connotations have helped guide the distinctions between morality and ethics.

So while they're closely related concepts, *morals* refer mainly to guiding principles, and *ethics* refer to specific rules and actions, or behaviors. A moral precept is an idea or opinion that's driven by a desire to be good. An *ethical code* is a set of rules that defines allowable actions or correct behavior. A person's idea of morals tends to be shaped by their surrounding environment (and sometimes their belief system). Moral values shape a person's ideas about right and wrong. They often provide the guiding idea behind ethical systems.

Ethics are distinct from *morals* in that they're much more practical. An ethical code doesn't have to be moral. It's just a set of rules for people to follow. Several professional organizations (like the American Bar Association and the American Medical Association) have created specific ethical codes for their respective fields. In other words, an ethical code has nothing to do with righteousness or a set of beliefs. It's a set of rules that are drafted by groups to ensure members stay out of trouble and act in a way that brings credit to the profession. Ethics aren't always moral and vice versa.

Omerta, for example, is a code of silence that developed among members of the Mafia. It was used to protect criminals from the police. This follows the rules of ethically-correct behavior for the organization, but it can also be viewed as wrong from a moral standpoint or the ethical system in law if the law is broken. A moral action can also be unethical. A lawyer who tells the court that his client is guilty may be acting out of a moral desire to see justice done, but this is deeply unethical because it violates the attorney-client privilege. Some moral principles are: Be honest, be loyal, be patient, be just and be generous. Some ethical principles are respect, fairness and integrity.

Comparing Morals with Ethics

Ethics	Morals
The guiding principle which individual or group decides what is good or bad	The beliefs of the individual as to what is right and wrong
General principles set by groups	Principles of right and wrong
Depends on the situation or context	Social or cultural norms
Governed by individuals/legal/profession	Differs in each culture/society
Can be abstract	Expressed in specific form of rules or statements
Applies to business and institutions	Does not specifically apply to businesses or institutions
Individuals have freedom to think or choose behavior	No choice

Susan Liautaud teaches ethics courses at Stanford University, serves as Chair of Council of the London School of Economics and Political Science, and is the founder of the nonprofit platform The Ethics Incubator. In her new book, *The Power of Ethics: How to Make Good Choices in a Complicated World.* She concludes:

- **Ethics are contagious.** "We see the same news headlines over and over: sexual misconduct, corporate malfeasance, misuse of our data, politicians' chronic lies, et cetera. We focus on eradicating unwanted behavior, but we often leave what drove the spreading of the behavior to fester and spur further trouble. While we can identify behavior that spreads COVID-19, for example, we have not sufficiently addressed the drivers of the underlying ethics, such as false information, fear, skewed economic incentives, failed leadership, and impunity. In short, the contagion of our ethics is inextricably linked to the contagion of societal challenges. But once we focus on identifying and dismantling these drivers and deploying them for good, we can break the cycle of reading about the same problems over and over."

- **There is no such thing as ethics without truth.** "I saw a story of a 69-year-old Dutch man who urged a court to let him change his legal age because he felt like he was 20 years younger. Thankfully, the court declined. Age is a fact, not a feeling or an opinion, and factual accuracy is the scaffolding of our society. It's the very foundation for human interaction and trust, and our decisions hinge on a truthful assessment of relevant information—for example, we grant privileges such as voting, drinking, driving, and marriage based on accurate age. So today's assault on truth threatens social relationships, democracy, and even ethics itself. We can do ethics in a world of wishful thinking all we want, but reality's truth will always come back to bite us—and have a real impact on real people."

CHAPTER 5

What Is Moral and Ethical Leadership?

"I am sure that in estimating every man's value either in private or public life, a pure integrity is the quality we take first into calculation, and that learning and talents are only the second."

—Thomas Jefferson

Oxford Dictionaries *defines "ethics" as: "Moral principles that govern a person's behavior or the conducting of an activity."*

The complexity, of course, comes about because many moral principles aren't universally held. We can all agree, I think, that it's morally wrong to kill and steal and suchlike, but on other issues, such as the ethics of animal testing, opinions differ based on religion, culture, and personal beliefs.

Sometimes one moral principle comes into conflict with another. You may prize freedom of speech, for example, but what if one of your employees uses that freedom to abuse another?

So ethical leadership means staying true to your moral principles, while also being aware of the complexity of some ethical issues and being sensitive to the differing views of your employees and managing the conflicts that may arise.

Unfortunately, ethics and leadership don't always go together. According to a study by the Institute of Leadership & Management:

- 63% of managers have been asked to do something contrary to their own ethical code.

- 43% have been told to behave in direct violation of their organization's own values statements.

- 9% have been asked to break the law.

The Benefits of Ethical Leadership

When the post mortems were conducted on various corporate and political scandals over the years, it became clear that the mistakes could've been avoided if strong ethical leadership had been in place and managers had questioned or prevented the wrongdoing before it escalated.

Studies have found practical, positive benefits too. For example, one experiment at Cornell University found that "ethical leadership was positively and significantly related to employee performance."

Another study published in *Science Direct* showed that ethical leadership made employees less likely to leave. Given the high cost of employee turnover, this is a significant benefit.

Although the topic of ethical leadership has long been considered by scholars, descriptive research on ethical leadership is relatively new. Some of the first formal investigations focused on defining ethical leadership from a descriptive perspective and were conducted by Linda K. Treviñob and colleagues. Their qualitative research revealed that ethical leaders were best described along two related dimensions: moral person and moral manager.

The moral person dimension refers to the qualities of the ethical leader as a person. Strong moral persons are honest and trustworthy. They demonstrate a concern for other people and are also seen as approachable. Employees can come to these individuals with problems and concerns, knowing that they will be heard. Moral persons have a reputation for being fair and principled. Lastly, moral persons are seen as consistently moral in both their personal and professional lives.

The moral manager dimension refers to how the leader uses the tools of the position of leadership to promote ethical conduct at work. Strong moral managers see themselves as role models in the workplace. They make ethics salient by modeling ethical conduct to their employees. Moral managers set and communicate ethical standards and use rewards and punishments to ensure those standards are followed. In sum, leaders who are moral managers "walk the talk" *and* "talk the walk," patterning their behavior and organizational processes to meet moral standards.

People who try to appear to be strong moral managers who are weak moral persons are likely to be seen as hypocrites, failing to practice what they preach. Hypocritical leaders talk about the importance of ethics, but their actions show them to be dishonest and unprincipled. Conversely, a strong moral person who is a weak moral manager runs the risk of being seen as an ethically "neutral" leader. That is, the leader is perceived as being silent on ethical issues, suggesting to employees that the leader does not really care about ethics.

Unethical Behavior Can Spread Among Employees

Emerging research has found that ethical leadership is related to important follower outcomes, such as employees' job satisfaction, organizational commitment, willingness to report problems to supervisors, willingness to put in extra effort on the job, voice behavior (i.e., expression of constructive suggestions intended to improve standard procedures), and perceptions of organizational culture and ethical climate. At the group level, supervisory ethical leadership is positively related to organizational citizenship behavior and psychological safety, and negatively related to workplace deviance.

Ethical leadership enhances followers' perceptions of important job characteristics such as autonomy and task significance, the latter mediating the relationship between ethical leadership and follower effort. At the highest levels of management, executive ethical leadership is positively related to perceived executive leadership team (ELT) effectiveness as well as optimism among members.

Traditional leadership literature has not described destructive leader behavior as "unethical"; however, the implication is clear. Unethical behavior involves acts that are illegal and/or are morally inappropriate to larger society. Dark side research has uncovered a variety of unethical leader acts. Various terms have evolved in the literature, such as abusive supervision, supervisor toxic leadership, and tyrannical leadership. Research shows these leaders are oppressive, abusive, manipulative, and calculatingly undermining. Their actions are perceived as intentional and harmful, and may be the source of legal action against employers. Therefore, by these measures, destructive leader behavior is unethical.

Unethical leadership transcends beyond the leaders' own behavior. In seeking to accomplish organizational goals, leaders can encourage corrupt and unethical acts within their organizations. For instance, a review of corporate scandals in *Fortune 100* corporations concluded that actions perpetrated by executives, boards of directors, and government officials were the primary cause of such transgressions.

Leaders can foster unethical behavior among followers without engaging in the behavior themselves and do so by way of rewards, condoning non-conformers, and ignoring unethical acts. Qualitative research shows leaders who reward short-term results, model aggressive and

Machiavellian behavior, do not punish followers' wrongdoing, end up promoting like-minded individuals, and heighten unethical behavior within organizations. Indeed, research shows employees engage in unethical acts to boost organizational performance or help the organization in some other way. Such embedded practices can insulate leaders from primary blame, essentially providing them "plausible deniability".

One of the most common and reprehensible defenses that unethical followers use when engaging in unethical (and/or immoral) behavior is that they were just "following orders" given by the leader(s).

The influence of an unethical, narcissistic sociopath like Donald Trump cannot be underestimated. During his presidency he has given the green light to thousands of leaders and followers throughout the country to act in unethical, amoral and immoral ways. "If the person at the top can do it, then it's okay for me too," many of them would argue.

The Lack of Self-Regulation

Self-regulation principles have also been used to explain why unethical leadership occurs. In particular, this approach draws from the social cognitive theory of moral thought and action which suggests that leaders may behave unethically because they disconnect themselves from moral standards and rationalize unethical treatment toward their employees. For example, researchers Marie S. Mitchell and her colleagues found leaders engaged in abusive behaviors and thought doing so was justified against employees who were poor performers.

Researchers Leanne S. Son Hing, and her colleagues found leaders with a strong social dominance orientation were more likely to engage in unethical behavior, particularly when followers were more agreeable; and/ or followers high in conservative authoritarianism, as evidenced more frequently with Republicans than with Democrats.

The important influence of emotions on ethical judgments can be traced as far back as Aristotle. Feelings inform us when things are not right—they act as ethical alarms. Rommel Salvador and Robert Folger highlight this point and discuss the role of emotions on ethical judgments with the human brain. Their review suggests emotions consciously and unconsciously influence ethical decision making and behavior. Understanding the role of emotions then is essential for furthering research on leadership and business ethics.

Emotional contagion is defined as an unconscious transfer of emotion, which fosters mimicry of another's emotional state. Research shows individuals who perceive their leaders displaying more positive than negative emotions experience more positive and less negative moods themselves. Groups with leaders who display positive emotions exhibit more coordination and expend less effort than groups with negatively affective leaders. Additionally, positive emotional displays from leaders influence followers' perceptions of their leader (e.g., effectiveness, motivational ability) and important outcomes, such as citizenship behavior and performance.

Leaders are also capable of inciting negative emotions among their followers and when they do these negative emotions are more vivid than positive emotions. In particular, employees recall more negative than positive events of their leaders, and the feelings associated with the negative memories are more intense than those experienced with positive memories. Negative emotional reactions to leaders can spread throughout an organization as emotional contagion, ultimately hurting the group's climate and heightening cynicism about the leader.

Emotional, attitudinal, and behavioral reactions to leaders' emotions have been generally explained by affective events theory and emotional transference principles. Leaders shape affective events within organizations and these events "transfer" the emotional state of followers. Events trigger emotional as well as impulsive behavioral reactions among employees. Over time, long-term attitudes can be affected. The influence of negative emotions can be even more impactful because negative emotions are felt with greater intensity compared to positive emotions.

Additionally, research on emotions may build an understanding of the consequences of ethical and unethical leadership. For instance, we expect ethical leadership will trigger more positive follower emotions (e.g., gratitude, awe, enthusiasm, empathy), whereas unethical leadership could affect more negative emotions (e.g., anger, fear, jealousy, selfishness). We also surmise that the relationship between (un)ethical leadership and follower (un)ethical behavior, would be moderated by the level of emotional contagion experienced and harnessed by the leader.

Further, research suggests the type and strength of the emotions evoked by followers will differentially influence their behavior. For instance, experienced anger or disgust (likely reactions to unethical leadership) may lead to employee unethical acts (e.g., retaliation, deviance), whereas experienced compassion or gratitude (likely reactions to ethical leadership) may influence employees to engage in ethical behavior (e.g., volunteerism, prosocial behavior).

Values congruence has explained the relationship between leader-follower cognitive moral development and follower attitudes. And, values congruence was found to mediate the relationship between charismatic leadership and workplace deviance. Work group values conflicts are associated with decreased member satisfaction, intention to remain, and commitment to the work group.

Leaders' values have been shown to uniquely shape the organization's environment. Research found that leaders embed their values into the framework of organizations by surrounding themselves with individuals who are similar to them. Indeed, research suggests the more followers align with their leaders, the more career success they experience.

On the other hand, diversity in moral values is different than other kinds of diversity in that individuals are less tolerant of moral diversity compared to demographic

71

diversity. Heterogeneity in ethical values within an organization could work against attempts to foster an effective ethics and compliance program based on shared values. However, more research is needed to determine the relationship between ethical values fit/misfit, leadership, and important ethical outcomes in organizations.

Katarina Katja Mihelič and her colleagues, in their published research on ethical leadership argue "ethical leadership can be viewed in terms of healing and energizing powers of love, recognizing that leadership is a reciprocal relation with followers. The leader's mission is to serve and support and his passion for leading comes from compassion."

To be able to influence followers' ethical behavior, leaders must communicate ethical standards and continually evaluate real examples. This means that solely writing a code of ethics is not a sufficient step towards implementation of ethical behavior in organizations. Ethics should be ingrained in each and every pore of organizational life. Ethical leaders are perceived as people who do not tolerate ethical lapses, they rather discipline people for wrong behavior. Research found that to be perceived as an ethical leader one has to be honest, trustworthy, show credibility and demonstrate integrity, needs to walk the ethical talk, and is courageous and strong.

A leader's character influences his ethical performance, but poor character alone does not fully explain ethical lapses in corporations. However, it is true that a strong character plays an important role in effective self-leadership and in the process of leading others.

Leaders therefore must rely on their inner voice, inner compass that points them in the ethical direction. Stephen Covey addresses the issue of ethical leadership with the term "character ethics", that he understands not as of individual character, but of "principles that govern human effectiveness" being self-validating natural laws.

Ethical and Unethical leadership (Zanderer, 1992)

The Ethical Leader	The Unethical Leader
Is humble	Is arrogant and self-serving
Is concerned for the greater good	Excessively promotes self-interest
Is honest and straightforward	Practices deception
Honors commitments	Breaches agreements
Strives for fairness	Deals unfairly
Takes responsibility	Shifts blames to others
Show respect for each person	Diminishes others' dignity
Encourages and develops others	Neglects follower development
Serves others	Withholds help and support
Shows courage to stand up for what is right	Lacks courage to confront unjust acts

The traits that CEOs most often attribute to ethical leaders are honesty, trustworthiness and integrity. Trust is associated with credibility, consistency and predictability in relationships, honesty is the crucial element needed in a trust-based relationship. Ethical leaders treat people right, have a high level of moral development and play fair. The leader who is honest with and about himself and with others inspires trust that encourages followers to take responsibility. For more than a decade, leadership experts James Kouzes and Barry Posner have been asking employees around the world what they most value or want from a leader and what would it take for them to follow him willingly.

Without exception honesty (integrity, trustworthiness) is the first on the list. And how do employees know that leaders are (dis)honest? They observe the behavior and the consistency of behavior in similar conditions. If a leader constantly changes his behavior, followers perceive him as unpredictable, unreliable, and therefore unworthy of trusting. Another thing that undermines trust is if a leader espouses one set of values (the way he should behave) and actively promotes them, whereas personally practices another set.

Harvard Business School Professor Joseph L. Baradarcco believes that over the course of a career a leader needs to embrace a more complex code of ethical behavior compared to the one learned in childhood and adolescence. He contends that real morality is not binary. Rather it emerges in many shades of gray. That is the reason why leaders need ethical codes that are as varied, complex and indeed subtle as the situation they face. Consequently, leaders need to embrace a wider set of human values and constantly evaluate their basic values.

Ethics and Integrity

Today one of the traits most cited as required in order to exercise effective leadership is integrity. In fact, a crucial point that distinguishes a Fortune 500 organization from its competitors is the integrity of profit making and other resource allocation practice by managers and owners.

The leaders who demonstrate integrity are honest with themselves and others. They lead by example and expect as much of others as they do of themselves. They take responsibility.

Raytheon's CEO, Dan Burhnam, shared his view on integrity within ethical leaders: "The CEO must be the chief ethics officer of the firm. He or she cannot delegate integrity...The CEO must make everyone understand that the organization's future is dependent on its reputations. The organization has to be personal, human and individual...If unethical behavior is uncovered, it's important to act swiftly and decisively."

Evaluation of Ethical Leadership (Yukl & Yukl, 2002)

Criterion	Ethical Leadership	Unethical Leadership
Use of leader power and influence	Serves followers and the organization	Serves self and career objectives
Handling diverse interests of multiple stakeholders	Attempts to balance and integrates	Favors coalition partners who offer the most benefits
Development of a vision for the organization	Based on follower input about their needs, values and ideas	Attempts to sell a personal vision as the only way to succeed
Integrity of leader behavior	Acts consistent with espoused values	Does what is expedient to attain personal objectives
Risk taking	Is willing to take personal risks and make necessary decisions	Avoids decisions or actions that involve personal risk to the leader
Communication of relevant information	Makes a complete disclosure of problems and actions	Uses deception and distortion to bias follower perceptions
Response to criticism and dissent by followers	Encourages critical evaluation to find better solutions	Discourages and suppresses criticism or dissent
Development of others	Uses coaching, mentoring and training to develop followers	De-emphasizes development to keep followers weak and dependent on the leader

Max Bazerman, the author of *Better, Not Perfect: A Realist's Guide to Maximum Sustainable Goodness*, and an article in the *Harvard Business Review*, "A New Model for Ethical Leadership," argues that leaders "should be guided by the goal of creating the most value for society. Moving beyond a set of simple ethical rules ('Don't lie,' 'Don't cheat'), this perspective—rooted in the work of the philosophers Jeremy Bentham, John Stuart Mill, and Peter Singer—provides the clarity needed to make a wide variety of important managerial decisions."

Bazerman's perspective is a utilitarian one which means "maximizing aggregate well-being and minimizing aggregate pain, goals that are helped by pursuing efficiency in decision-making, reaching moral decisions without regard for self-interest, and avoiding tribal behavior (such as nationalism or in-group favoritism)."

Bazerman cites the work of psychologist Daniel Kahneman and colleagues who asked these two questions:

1. How much would you pay to save 2,000 migrating birds from drowning in uncovered oil ponds?

2. How much would you pay to save 200,000 migrating birds from drowning in uncovered oil ponds?

Their research shows that people who are asked the first question offer about the same amount as do people who are asked the second question. Of course, if our goal is to create as much value as possible, a difference in the number of birds should affect how much we choose to pay. This illustrates the limitations of our ethical thinking and suggests that improving ethical decision-making requires deliberately making rational decisions that maximize value rather than going with one's gut.

Bazerman says that the concept of bounded rationality, which is core to the field of behavioral economics, sees managers as wanting to be rational but influenced by biases and other cognitive limitations that get in the way. Scholars of decision-making don't expect people to be fully rational, but they argue that we should aspire to be so in order to better align our behavior with our goals.

In the ethics domain we struggle with bounded ethicality—systematic cognitive barriers that prevent us from being as ethical as we wish to be. By adjusting our personal goals from maximizing benefit for ourselves (and our organizations) to behaving as ethically as possible, we can establish a sort of North Star to guide us.

We may never reach it, but it can inspire us to create more good, increasing well-being for everyone. Aiming in that direction can move us toward increasing what Bazerman calls maximum sustainable goodness: the level of value creation that we can realistically achieve.

Bazerman argues that far too many executives unconsciously overlook wrongdoing if it benefits them or the company. Trying to create more value requires that we confront our cognitive limitations.

Daniel Kahneman's book *Thinking, Fast and Slow*, describes how we have two very different modes of decision-making.

System 1 is our intuitive system, which is fast, automatic, effortless, and emotional. We make most decisions using System 1. System 2 is our more deliberative thinking, which is slower, conscious, effortful, and logical. We come much closer to rationality when we use System 2. The philosopher and psychologist Joshua Greene has developed a parallel two-system view of ethical decision-making: an intuitive system and a more deliberative one. The deliberative system leads to more ethical behaviors.

One reason that intuition and emotions tend to dominate decision-making is that we typically think about our options one at a time, Bazerman says. When evaluating one option (such as a single job offer or a single potential charitable contribution), we lean on System 1 processing. But when we compare multiple options, our decisions are more carefully considered and less biased, and they create more value. We donate on the basis of emotional tugs when we consider charities in isolation; but when we make comparisons across charities, we tend to think more about where our contribution will do the most good.

Similarly, in research with the economists Iris Bohnet and Alexandra van Geen, Bazerman found that when people evaluate job candidates one at a time, System 1 thinking kicks in, and they tend to fall back on gender stereotypes. For example, they are more likely to hire men for mathematical tasks. But when they compare two or more applicants at a time, they focus more on job-relevant criteria, are more ethical (less sexist), hire better candidates, and obtain better results for the organization.

The second strategy involves adapting what the philosopher John Rawls called the *veil of ignorance*. Rawls argued that if you thought about how society should be structured without knowing your status in it (rich or poor, man or woman, black or white)—that is, behind a veil of ignorance—you would make fairer, more-ethical decisions. Indeed, recent empirical research by Karen Huang and Joshua Greene shows that those who make ethical decisions behind a veil of ignorance do create more value. They are more likely, for instance, to save more lives with scarce resources (say, medical supplies), because they allocate them in less self-interested ways.

Bazerman observes, "Whatever your organization, I'm guessing it's quite socially responsible in some ways but less so in others, and you may be uncomfortable with the latter. Most organizations get higher ethical marks on some dimensions than on others. I know companies whose products make the world worse, but they have good diversity and inclusion policies. I know others whose products make the world better, but they engage in unfair competition that destroys value in their business ecosystem. Most of us are ethically inconsistent as well. Otherwise honest people may view deception in negotiation with a client or a colleague as completely acceptable. If we care about the value or harm we create, remembering that we're likely to be ethical in some domains and unethical in others can help us identify where change might be most useful."

Bazerman cites the case of Andrew Carnegie who gave away 90% of his wealth—about $350 million—to endow an array of institutions, including Carnegie Hall, the Carnegie Foundation, and more than 2,500 libraries. But he also engaged in miserly, ineffective, and probably criminal behavior as a business leader, such as destroying the union at his steel mill in Homestead, Pennsylvania.

More recently, Bazerman observes, this divide between good and bad is evident in the behavior of the Sackler family. The Sacklers have made large donations to art galleries, research institutes, and universities, including Harvard, with money earned through the family business, Purdue Pharma, which made billions by marketing—and, most experts argue, over-marketing—the prescription painkiller OxyContin. By 2018 OxyContin was responsible for the deaths of more than 15,000 Americans, and has become a national health crisis, yet the Sacklers took no personal responsibility, but were happy to receive the millions of dollars from the sale of the dangerous drug.

Then there's the case of one of founders of the American Republic, Thomas Jefferson. He wrote that "all men are created equal," in the Declaration of Independence and yet enslaved more than 600 people over the course of his life.

Bazerman argues that leaders can do far more than just make their own behavior more ethical. Because they are responsible for the decisions of others as well as their own, they can dramatically multiply the amount of good they do by encouraging others to be better. As a leader, think about how you can influence your colleagues with the norms you set and the decision-making environment you create.

People follow the behavior of others, particularly those in positions of power and prestige. Employees in organizations with ethical leaders can be expected to behave more ethically themselves.

Leaders can also create more value and act more ethically by shaping the environment in which others make decisions. In their book *Nudge,* Richard Thaler and Cass Sunstein describe how we can design the "architecture" surrounding choices to prompt people to make value-creating decisions. Perhaps the most common type of nudge involves changing the default choice that decision-makers face. A famous nudge encourages organ donation in some European nations by enrolling citizens in the system automatically, letting them opt out if they wish. The program increased the proportion of people agreeing to be donors from less than 30% to more than 80%.

Bazerman contends that "new ethical challenges confront us daily, from what algorithm to create for self-driving cars to how to allocate scarce medical supplies during a pandemic. As technology creates amazing ways to improve our lives, our environmental footprint becomes a bigger concern. Many countries struggle with how to act when their leaders reject System 2 thinking and even truth itself. And in too many countries, finding collective value is no longer a national goal. We all crave ethical direction from our leaders."

CHAPTER 6

Wisdom in Leadership

"Yesterday I was clever, so I wanted to change the world. Today I am wise, so I am changing myself."

—Rumi

I would argue that wisdom is inextricably tied to moral and ethical behavior

The Oxford English Dictionary defines wisdom as "capacity of judging rightly in matters relating to life and conduct; soundness of judgment in the choice of means and ends; sometimes, less strictly, sound sense, especially in practical affairs: opposite to folly;" also "knowledge (especially of a high or abstruse kind); enlightenment, learning, erudition." Wisdom is the ability to think and act using knowledge, experience, understanding, common sense and insight. Wisdom is associated with attributes such as unbiased judgment, compassion, experiential self-knowledge, self-transcendence and non-attachment, and virtues such as ethics and benevolence.

Business gurus Robert I. Sutton and Andrew Hargadon define the "attitude of wisdom" as "acting with knowledge while doubting what one knows". In social and psychological sciences, several distinct approaches to wisdom exist, with major advances made in the last two decades with respect to operationalization and measurement of wisdom as a psychological construct. Wisdom is the capacity to have foreknowledge of something, to know the consequences (both positive and negative) of all the available courses of action, and to yield or take the options with the most advantage either for the present or future.

Historical, Cultural and Philosophical Perspectives

Sapience has also been used to define wisdom and is closely related to the term "sophia" often defined as "transcendent wisdom", "ultimate reality", or the "ultimate truth of things." The sapiential perspective of wisdom is said to lie in the heart of every religion, where it is often acquired through intuitive knowing. This type of wisdom is described as going beyond mere practical wisdom and includes self-knowledge, interconnectedness, conditioned origination of mind-states and other deeper understandings of subjective experience. This type of wisdom can also lead to the ability of an individual to act with appropriate judgment, a broad understanding of situations and greater appreciation/compassion towards other living beings.

The word *sapience* is derived from the Latin *sapientia*, meaning "wisdom". The corresponding verb *sapere* has the original meaning of "to taste", hence "to perceive, to discern" and "to know"; its present participle *sapiens* was chosen by

Carl Linnaeus for the Latin binomial for the human species, *Homo Sapiens*.

The origin of wisdom may be traced to the time when humans began to reflect on their own thoughts. With its long trail of historical nuances accumulated throughout the centuries across different regions of the world, it is not surprising that wisdom is one of our most enduring and yet elusive concepts.

Ancient texts, tablets and stories of the importance of wisdom in mythology, religions and histories is mentioned in ancient civilizations for over 3000 years in Sumerian, Egyptian, Greek, Hebrew, Roman, Indian and Asian cultures.

Previous research has defined wisdom exclusively from a Western perspective focusing on the analytic mode. The dominant Western tradition understood wisdom from a "split" perspective and defined wisdom exclusively as a high level of analytical skill.

The fact that the Western intellectual tradition has emphasized literacy and logic and has produced numerous writings that continue to be influential today may also have contributed to the idea that wisdom is not necessarily a personal quality but a general property or a type of knowledge that can be acquired.

In contrast, the Eastern philosophies such as Hinduism, Buddhism, and Taoism emphasize the "non-split" perspective and value both the analytical and experiential or intuitive components as two sides of the same coin. Those views hold that having knowledge is important, it is also necessary that a wise person has cognitive, emotional, interpersonal, and intuitive understanding.

With an increasing popularity of Buddhism after Buddha's death, relevant manuscripts were reinterpreted and rewritten numerous times in various scholastic traditions. As a consequence, the meaning of wisdom as divine knowledge was transformed from a religious and mystical knowing to a more practical and logical knowledge.

For this reason, the concept of wisdom came to be associated with less of an emphasis on inclusivity and personal experience involving cognition, emotion, intuition, and other psychological processes, and more of an emphasis on knowledge per se, with accentuated with analytical and practical properties.

Current Perspectives on Wisdom

In the fields of psychology and business management, wisdom remains one of those constructs used freely in everyday conversation, but sometimes shunned by, and often used inconsistently in, academic circles. So too, discussions about the characteristics of great leaders often focus on their personality and cognitive accomplishments and rarely make reference to their wisdom.

Unlike personal wisdom, general wisdom is a type of analytical tool used primarily to solve general problems of others. As such, a person with general wisdom is detached from the situation with minimal emotional involvement so that he or she can draw a logical and practical conclusion.

In the ultimate form, general wisdom can well be a "collectively anchored product or extensive written materials, such as the Holy Bible or legal texts, that are "too large and complex to be stored in one individual's mind". Researchers P. B. Baltes and Ursula Staudinger thus claim that individuals can never attain wisdom per se but should simply be regarded as "weak carriers of wisdom".

Particularly when virtually anyone can have access to an infinite amount of information and knowledge, literally at his/her fingertips, a person with a huge information database does not seem particularly wise. To put it differently, one still has to know what to google before one actually Googles.

As Monika Ardelt states, "wisdom-related knowledge has to be realized by an individual through a reflection on personal experiences to be called wisdom and that the wisdom-related knowledge that is written down in texts remains theoretical or intellectual knowledge until a person re-transforms it into wisdom".

Other researchers and theorists have proposed wisdom must be as a result of the practice of reflection; wisdom refers to a person's ability to understand life, and comprehend the significance and deeper meaning of phenomena and events with regard to intrapersonal and interpersonal matters. The affective dimension of wisdom is about improving one's affective emotions and demeanor toward others and tends to increase sympathetic and compassionate love. Wisdom means looking at many different perspectives and developing one's self-awareness and self-insight; and wisdom means understanding the motivations of one's own and other people's behavior.

Wisdom and Ethical Behavior

In their research Harvard professors Donna Hicks and Sandra Waddock examined the role wisdom and dignity play in developing ethical business leaders. They define wisdom as the integration of moral imagination (the good), systems understanding (the true) and aesthetic sensibility (the beautiful) into decisions, actions and practices in the service of a better world. They say that dignity is our inherent value, worth and vulnerability, a core aspect of human that each of us is born with and are at the core of ethical leadership.

Moral imagination is the ability to see the ethical issues embedded in situations and decisions, or what philosophers have long called "the good." Moral imagination has been linked to systems understanding (actually, systems thinking), which means a reasonably accurate perspective on the system as a whole, or what we can call "the true." The third element of wisdom is aesthetic sensibility, or the ability to appreciate the design and aesthetic elements of a situation, decision, organization, or whatever is affected, that is, what philosophers call "the beautiful."

Hicks and Waddock argue that the integration of these three elements alone is insufficient to qualify as wisdom; they must be put into the service of building a better world to qualify as wise, since acts and decisions that make the world worse cannot be justified as wise decisions. Further, there is an explicit link to dignity in this definition, as wisdom enables leaders to address what needs to be healed most in the world today—shattered dignity. It is not just the dignity of people that matters in this context, but equally importantly, the dignity of our enterprises, institutions, nations, and the very planet itself.

As an interesting side note here, President Biden made multiple references to restoring dignity to America as the biggest and most important challenge the nation and its leaders face.

Dignity they define as our inherent value, worth, and vulnerability. All human beings are born worthy but at the same time, are vulnerable to having one's worth violated, just as we are all born vulnerable to physical injuries. Understanding dignity requires us to treat this core aspect of our humanity with as much care and attention as the physical aspects of our being. It also means that dignity needs to be accorded to our institutions and to the planet that supports us.

Dignity is also different from respect. It is a common misconception to treat them as the same. While dignity is something we all have by virtue of our birth—all human beings are born worthy— respect, conversely, needs to be earned. When people demand to be respected, what they really mean is that they want to be treated as something of value. We have to do something to earn respect whereas dignity is just part of our DNA. Respect is something we reserve for people who have done something admirable and inspiring.

Psychologist Judith Glück, reflecting the views of Robert Sternberg, has long been arguing that we need to educate our children for more than just intelligence and knowledge—we need to figure out how to foster wisdom. Wisdom, she contends, goes beyond intelligence and knowledge in that it includes aspects of self-reflection, openness, compassion, and morality. In other words, she says, it is what enables people to use their intelligence for the sake of a common good.

Education affects wisdom implying that education may promote wisdom in young years and support its maintenance later in life. These quantitative findings are complemented by two qualitative studies that looked at how wisdom develops as people reflect upon life experiences. They found that a person's social environment plays an important role in enabling them to gain wisdom from an experience. The role of others in the development of wisdom is, in fact, a highly important and understudied area.

They found that people they studied often felt they had gained wisdom from difficult and fundamental events and that wiser participants showed more growth-oriented forms of self-reflection in thinking about the events.

According to some studies, wisdom increases with age, stays stable, increases, then decreases depending on how you measure it. Some researchers found that wisdom as a whole showed an inverse U-shaped curve, but there were different curves for the three dimensions of wisdom. But who can we turn to for wisdom in the human world? In studies in which participants were asked to nominate individuals that they thought wise, the average age for nominees was about 55 or 60. Nominees in one specific study included such old-timers as Gandhi, Confucius, Socrates, Queen Elizabeth, and the Pope. Clearly, the public believes that with age comes wisdom.

Although wisdom can arise from difficult experiences, it also helps people to cope with them. In a quantitative study of almost 1,000 older adults, they found that wisdom served as an effective buffer against the negative effects of adverse events on well-being. In other words, wiser individuals showed higher well-being than other people as they were coping with a difficult experience. Together, these studies illustrate that we need to combine qualitative and quantitative methods to understand both the larger effects— or predictors—of wisdom and how exactly wisdom manifests itself—or develops—as people deal with and learn from life.

Taking a cultural perspective on wisdom is important in many ways. One is that the state of our planet today requires us to find ways to cross national and cultural boundaries— to learn how to take all of humanity into account as we make decisions that shape our own and our children's future. Climate change, global inequality, and the rise of national and religious radicalism can only be countered if nations act in concert and try to find long-term sustainable ways of supporting one another.

Yet what is happening today in the United States, and many other places seems to be heading in exactly the opposite direction. We see on a daily basis behavior by adults that is unethical, amoral and unwise. How can that not affect children?

How can we teach our children to think in less selfish or in-group-focused ways and to find balanced solutions to global problems that optimize outcomes for as many as possible?

Psychologist Igor Grossman of the University of Waterloo argues that understanding wisdom involves taking the wise off their pedestal, and seeing wisdom as a set of processes that we can all tap into, with the right attitude, and in the right context. Grossman and his colleagues published their research in *Social Psychological and Personality Science* which used a diary approach to gauge people's wisdom in response to everyday problems, and the results showed that there is more variation in one person's wisdom from one situation to the next, than there is variation in the average wisdom between people. Wisdom, it seems, is more of a state than a personal trait.

The Wise, Ethical Leader

An ethical leader understands the central role that dignity and wisdom play in our lives and relationships and is educated in all matters related to dignity, and to wisdom. Although we are all born worthy, we are not necessarily born knowing how to act worthy, nor how to treat others as if they are worthy. An ethical leader recognizes that this fundamental aspect of what it means to be human has to be learned and practiced, just as wisdom is gained through effort and experience. Gaining dignity, knowledge, and wisdom requires effort and commitment—neither comes naturally.

Wise and ethical leaders treat others as if they had intrinsic worth, that is, as whole persons worthy of care, with integrity in and of themselves, who need to be valued not for what they can do for the leader but simply because they are. Wise leaders, that is, recognize the inherent dignity in others, no matter who or where they are.

Wise leaders also treat the world around them, nature, and our planet Earth, the same way. That is, wise leaders recognize the intrinsic worth and value of Earth and value it for that worth, not because its resources can be exploited for personal or company gain. That attitude is very different from treating others—employees, for example, as means to the end of making money, or treating natural resources as something that should be exploited simply for material or wealth gains.

The difference means that people and the world around us are treated as wholes that are worthy of being cared for in and of themselves, not just because they are the means to greater wealth or subjects of exploitation, a fundamental ethical tenet. In recognizing the integrity of the world around us and that of other people, wise and ethical leaders treat both people and the planet as having intrinsic worth, and the quality of dignity.

The word integrity itself is worth reflecting on in this context, for it has multiple meanings relevant to the discussion of wise and ethical leadership. One important definition of integrity is being honest and having strong moral principles, (i.e., a sound ethical base), which relates directly to the idea of wise leadership as we conceive it. This definition relates integrity to truthfulness. In businesses, for example, we typically hope to see integrity—truthfulness—in a company's accounting statements, and we would hope to also see such integrity in the company's leaders and employees, its products or services, and its relationships with various stakeholders.

If we conceive a wise business leader as embodying the three elements of moral imagination, systems understanding, and aesthetic sensibility in the service of a better world, the importance of integrity in all of its definitions becomes clearer. Wise leaders under this definition understand that their decisions and acts have moral and ethical consequences, and are able to see what the consequences of those actions are likely to be.

Wisdom, in one sense, is the by-product of making all of these connections. It means recognizing not only our own dignity, but also the dignity of others and of something or things greater than ourselves. These things "greater than ourselves" could be organizations, communities, societies, nations, or, for many, a higher power or consciousness of some sort.

A wise leader first and foremost understands the importance of treating people as if they matter and has incorporated the following elements of dignity into a daily practice:

- **Acceptance of others' identity**: Approach people as neither inferior nor superior to you; give others the freedom to express their authentic selves without fear of being negatively judged; interact without prejudice or bias, accepting how race, religion, gender, class, sexual orientation, age, disability, etc. are at the core of their identities. Assume they all have integrity.

- **Recognition:** Validate others for their talents, hard work, thoughtfulness, and help; be generous with praise; give credit to others for their contributions, ideas, and experience.

- **Acknowledgment**: Give people your full attention by listening, hearing, validating, and responding to their concerns and what they have been through.

- **Inclusion:** Make others feel that they belong at all levels of relationship (family, community, organization, nation).

- **Safety:** Put people at ease at two levels: physically, where they feel free of bodily harm; and psychologically, where they feel free of concern about being shamed or humiliated, that they feel free to speak without fear of retribution.

- **Fairness:** Treat people justly, with equality, and in an evenhanded way, according to agreed on laws and rules.

- **Independence:** Empower people to act on their own behalf so that they feel in control of their lives and experience a sense of hope and possibility.

- **Understanding:** Believe that what others think matters; give them the chance to explain their perspectives, express their points of view; actively listen to understand them.

- **Benefit of the Doubt:** Treat people as trustworthy; start with the premise that others have good motives and are acting with integrity.

- **Accountability:** Take responsibility for your actions; if you have violated the dignity of another, apologize; make a commitment to change hurtful behaviors.

Equipped with this knowledge of dignity—how to treat people in a way that honors their inherent value and vulnerability—wise and ethical leaders can not only provide a pleasant environment for people to work, but also give them an opportunity to grow and flourish. As Johan Goethe reminds us, "Treat people as they want to be and you help them become what they are capable of being."

Wise leaders do far more than run a company and manage people. They know how to bring out the best in people and foster their development, they foster purpose and meaningfulness in the workplace, and they treat others with dignity. They help others heal themselves—and they do much the same for the organizations and world around us. When employees feel that their dignity is honored in all the ways described above, they do not have to waste precious time worrying about their worth and value to the organization. They are open to learning and expanding their view of the world.

Finally, wise leadership appears in the awareness of and coping with the personal limitations. Thus, wisdom recommends the abandonment of elitist individualism or domination e.g., through exploring the limits of one's own knowledge and seeking out the advice of others. Also, the virtue of humility, a commitment to life-long learning in a transformational and deep way and preparing a successor are important features of wise leadership.

CHAPTER 7

The Humility Connection

"Be gentle and you can be bold; be frugal and you can be liberal; avoid putting yourself before others and you can become a leader among men."

—Laozi

The research on moral and ethical leaders point to those who are honest and humble.

The more honesty and humility employees may have, the higher their job performance, as rated by the employees' supervisor. That's the new finding from a Baylor University study published in the journal *Personality and Individual Differences* that found the honesty-humility personality trait was a unique predictor of job performance.

"Researchers already know that integrity can predict job performance and what we are saying here is that humility and honesty are also major components in that," said Dr. Wade Rowatt, associate professor of psychology and neuroscience at Baylor, who helped lead the study. "This study shows that those who possess the combination of honesty and humility have better job performance. In fact, we found that humility and honesty not only correspond with job performance, but it predicted job performance above and beyond any of the other five personality traits like agreeableness and conscientiousness."

Humble leaders are more effective and better liked, according to a study published in the *Academy of Management Journal*. "Leaders of all ranks view admitting mistakes, spotlighting follower strengths and modelling teachability as being at the core of humble leadership" says Bradley Owens, assistant professor of organization and human resources at the University at Buffalo School of Management. A follow-up study published in the journal *Organization Science*, using data from more than 700 employees and 218 leaders, confirmed that leader humility is associated with more learning-oriented teams, more engaged employees and lower voluntary employee turnover.

In an article in the *Harvard Business Review* entitled "Level 5 Leadership: The Triumph of Humility and Fierce Resolve," leadership expert Jim Collins argues the best leaders exhibit humility, shunning public adulation and are never boastful. In a widely read *Harvard Business Review* publication, Collins explained that the personal humility of Level 5 Leaders was typified by: A compelling modesty about their accomplishments; quiet determination rather than charisma; ambition focused on the company rather than self; willingness to accept personal responsibility for failures; and acknowledgment of the role of others in achieving success.

There's a clear connection between moral and ethical behavior in leaders and their humility, according to F.O

Walumbwa, and J. Schaubroeck writing in the *Journal of Applied Psychology*. They conclude, "Leaders who are humble in their character and model humility in their actions, create the opposite kind of environment to that of the amoral unethical leader. This environment is grounded in respect, tolerance, and outcomes that are mutually beneficial for the firm and for the individual. Leaders who are good role models tend to radiate positivity, and instead of spawning a downward spiral, they create an upward spiral that elevates pro-social employee behaviors."

Mark R. Leary and Chloe C. Banker, argue in their book, *A Critical Examination and Reconceptualization of Humility*, "In contexts that operate as meritocracies, people who are good at something or who possess exceptional characteristics are entitled to preferential treatment within the domain of their expertise and accomplishments. The best athletes should get more playing time, the best employees should receive larger salaries, the best actors should win more awards, and so on. "

"The good leaders do the best thing in the prevailing situation whereas the great leaders do the right thing in any situation irrespective of the effects and outcomes."

—Professor M.S. Rao, Ph.D

Jennifer Cole Wright in her edited book, *Humility*, says, "The central problem with low humility is not that people think that they are better than others. People low in humility expect others to treat them as special; try to reap social benefits that they don't deserve; and their sense of entitlement leads them to behave in self-centered ways that disadvantage other people."

In contrast, humble people who do not put themselves above others, or expect preferential treatment, or think they are entitled to a disproportionate share of any benefits, and are more likely to treat others in an egalitarian, respectful, and fair manner, Wright argues.

All theorists agree that humility is associated with an array of prosocial behaviors, and studies support this connection. For example, humility is associated with gratitude, willingness to help others empathy forgiveness and success in working and communicating with others In close relationships, humble people display greater skill at conflict resolution and are more likely to make sacrifices for others and they display more trust, greater cooperation, and less conflict.

Researchers Yanhan Zhu and colleagues studied the relationship between humble leadership and employee resilience and productivity and concluded: Humble leaderships can be defined as: a leadership style in which a leader evaluates him/herself and subordinates through a multifaceted and objective lens, appreciating subordinates' positive worth, strengths, and contributions. It contains three behavioral components: (a) a willingness to acknowledge one's limits and mistakes; (b) shining a spotlight on employees' contributions and strengths; and (c) keeping openness to advice, ideas, and feedback.

Edgar H. Schein and Peter A. Schein in their research and published study, *Humble Leadership: The Power of Relationships, Openness and Trust,* argue that the growing complexity of the modern world requires stronger workplace relationships in order to accomplish tasks. They argue the pace of change in the world is increasing in just about every context.

The authors argue that the changing world necessitates humble leadership due to the changing nature of work:

- Leadership will become more about *context* and *process* rather than *content* and *expertise.*

- Humble Leadership can help overcome unconscious biases, segregation, and exclusion.

- Individual abuse of power is tempting. Humble leaders have a better track record of resisting the abuse of power in comparison with leaders with low humility.

- Humble leadership can help facilitate the movement toward agile organizations.

The authors make the salient point that the workplace now puts a premium on so-called "soft-skills" and experimental learning, and is moving away from authoritarian and one-size fits all training and development. They say that it's the leader's responsibility to foster those dynamics correctly by introducing the right tasks at the right time and at the right pace. A humble leader's effectiveness will depend on how well you can incorporate soft skills into the group dynamic so your group can accomplish even its most complex goals.

Humble leaders are more effective and better liked, according to a study published in the *Academy of Management Journal.* "Leaders of all ranks view admitting mistakes, spotlighting follower strengths and modelling "teachability" as being at the core of humble leadership" says Bradley Owens, assistant professor of organization and human resources at the University at Buffalo School of Management. A follow-up study published in the journal *Organization Science,* using data from more than 700 employees and 218 leaders, confirmed that leader humility is associated with more learning-oriented teams, more engaged employees and lower voluntary employee turnover.

The more honesty and humility an employee may have, the higher their job performance, as rated by the employees' supervisor according to a Baylor University study published in the journal *Personality and Individual Differences* by Wade Rowatt, associate professor of psychology and neuroscience. He found humility was a unique predictor of job performance.

Amy Y. Ou and her colleagues at Arizona State University published a study in *Administrative Science Quarterly,* examined the leadership traits associated with Confucianism. Those traits include self-awareness, openness to feedback, and a focus on the greater good and others' welfare, as opposed to dwelling on oneself. Ou and her colleagues argue the self-awareness of humble leaders enables them to be open-minded and willing to learn, to appreciate both their own strengths and weaknesses as well as those of others, and to transcend the self in the pursuit of a higher and more significant objective while continuing to improve.

They concluded "Accordingly, humility provides integration of both high self-knowledge and low self-focus in terms of identifying personal priorities about goal achievement." They contend humble leaders' "life pursuits are less about themselves than about the larger community, the greater whole, moral principles, or ultimate universal truth."

In an article in the *Harvard Business Review* entitled "Level 5 Leadership: The Triumph of Humility and Fierce Resolve," leadership expert Jim Collins argues the best leaders exhibit humility, compelling modesty, shunning public adulation and are never boastful. In a widely read *Harvard Business Review* publication, Collins explained that the personal humility of Level 5 Leaders was typified by: A compelling modesty about their accomplishments; quiet determination rather than charisma; ambition focused on the company rather than self; willingness to accept personal responsibility for failures; and acknowledgment of the role of others in achieving success.

Joseph Folkman writes in a report, "How Do You Become an Effective Leader? Stay Humble," a follow up to a previous article on humble leaders in *Harvard Business Review*, argues "How do people make the judgment that a leader is arrogant or humble? Arrogant leaders don't parade around with a badge indicating they are conceited. Yet, there is a high degree of consensus within organizations about who is humble and who is arrogant. The reality is that there are a set of very predictable behaviors that send clear signals about an individual's humility or arrogance." Folkman studied 1,072 leaders and concluded the following:

- **Humble leaders are rated higher than arrogant leaders on an overall leadership effectiveness index**. A comparison of arrogant and humble leaders on an overall leadership effectiveness index composed of 54 behaviors that differentiate the most effective from the least effective leaders. Arrogant leaders were rated at the 34th percentile, while humble leaders were rated at the 66th percentile.

- **Humble leaders demonstrated that people are just as important as results**. The arrogant leader believes that results are the ultimate goal, and if a few people get negatively affected, that's just the cost of doing business. The humble leaders understand the balance of achieving while still being sensitive to individual needs. They also believe if you take care of people, they will be more engaged and dedicated, which will produce better results in the long run.

- **Humble leaders focused on gaining trust from others.** Humble leaders do everything they can to build up trust with others. They are more effective on the key levers that build trust, which are: creating positive relationships, consistently delivering on their promises, and providing expertise and good judgment.

- **Humble leaders believe that success comes from cooperation and collaboration.** The arrogant leader believes that they can accomplish goals on their own. They resist collaboration because they want all the credit for themselves. The humble leaders know that organizational success comes from people working together. They ask others for help and resist taking credit for the accomplishments of others.

- **Humble leaders are role models and walk their talk.** When humble leaders ask others to do something, they make sure they do it first. Arrogant leaders are okay with asking others to do what they do not do. They are fine with having a double standard, or perhaps they don't see it. In many ways, they act as though they are a privileged class where rules for others do not apply to them.

- **Humble leaders ask for and acts on feedback from others.** Humble leaders ask others for feedback and work hard to implement their suggestions for change. Arrogant leaders feel that they do not want or need feedback from others. In fact, they often feel that asking for feedback would signal a lack of confidence in themselves. Therefore, they resist asking.

- **Humble leaders resolve conflicts productively.** Arrogant leaders tend to create conflict with others. This is due, in part, to a belief that conflict is a good thing that fuels competitive energy from others.

Humble leaders feel that conflict creates a negative work environment and work hard to resolve conflicts.

- **Humble leaders give others honest feedback.** The arrogant leaders believe their job is to be the judge and let others know when they make mistakes. Their feedback is almost always negative and corrective. The humble leader realizes that honest feedback needs to reflect an individual's performance.

Folkman says these behaviors listed above represent the largest differences between arrogant and humble leaders. "Looking over the list," Folkman says, "it isn't difficult to realize why humble leaders win. In many ways, humble leaders believe that leadership is the ability to get work done through others. In contrast, arrogant leaders believe leadership is the ability to get work done by others."

Increasingly, scholars and practitioners have argued the need for today's leaders to approach their roles with more humility. As result of workplace complexity and fast changes requiring leader flexibility, recent leadership theories have begun to place greater emphasis on the bottom-up aspects of leadership. Some experts even argue for a need to change the very idea of leadership — what it is and how it works and even how people even know it when they see it.

Researchers have also suggested that leaders should move beyond the hero myth or "great man" theory of leadership by having leaders show their humanness by being open about their limitations in knowledge and experience, and focusing more on how followers influence the process of leadership.

More recently many scholars and experts have called for professionals and leaders in all professions to approach their roles with more humility. For example, for lawyers and judges, humility is important to effectively interpret the law and balance the ideals of justice and mercy. In medicine, competence and humility are seen as the two essential dimensions of medical professionalism. Humility has also been spot-lighted as important for political and military leaders, particularly in the current political climate.

Bottom-up, participative leadership lends itself to the inclusion of humble leadership. Although some advocate top-down strategic change approaches others are now arguing the need for organizations to learn to "grow strategy from below," seek bottom-up "small wins," as reflected in the agile leadership model.

There are several similarities between humble leadership theory and servant leader theory. Servant leaders view the development of followers as an end, in and of itself, not merely a means to reach the leader's or the organization's goals.

Leaders who humbly acknowledge they do not need to be the master of all skills and communicating to others they have much to contribute in achieving an optimal result also builds organizational commitment and increases trust in the leader argue researchers Robert S. Dennis and Mihal Bocarnea. Not only does accurate self-knowledge recognize one's own values, they argue, but humble leaders fully recognize the importance of others' values and priorities — including the big picture capacity to pursue a better future that can come from collaborative action, and the necessity of creating strong partnerships with others to achieve that optimal future.

"In looking for people to hire, look for three qualities: Integrity, intelligence, and energy. And if they don't have the first, the other two will kill you."

— **Warren Buffett**

CHAPTER 8

How to Deal with an Amoral or Unethical Leader

"Ethics is about how we meet the challenge of doing the right thing, when that will cost more than we want to pay."

The Josephson Institute of Ethics

The Abusive Boss

Abusive bosses may retain their positions by taking superficial steps to repair their social images following outbursts, without acting meaningfully to change their behaviors, according to research led by a University of Wyoming business management expert.

Shawn McClean, an assistant professor in UW's College of Business, joined colleagues from the University of Iowa, the University of Nebraska-Lincoln and Texas A&M University in conducting the research, which appears in the journal *Personnel Psychology* and *Harvard Business Review*.

"Our study shows that supervisors are often driven by simply repairing their social image rather than making genuine amends and changing their behavior," McClean says. "As a result, employees may seemingly forgive abusive supervisors who try to 'fake nice' after abusive behavior, thus reinforcing the cycle of abuse."

Rather than take steps to genuinely repair damage caused by their abusive behavior, such as offering sincere apologies, many of the bosses were more concerned about repairing their social images, the researchers found. The bosses did small favors for employees with the express purpose of getting employees to view them more favorably, while also engaging in self-promoting behaviors, such as highlighting how hard they work or showcasing past successes.

"Consequently, even though abusive bosses may appear on the surface to be considerate to their victims following one of their abusive episodes, the bosses in our study reported behavior that was instead a superficial attempt at impression management," the researchers wrote, "as a result, toxic bosses were not likely to change their ways, mainly because their focus was on covering up their bad behavior through manipulative ingratiation and self-promotion behaviors, not on actually changing their toxic behaviors."

The researchers suggest that breaking the cycle of self-centered, manipulative and uncivil behavior by bosses requires organizational leaders to implement zero-tolerance policies for toxic supervisory behavior — and adhere to those policies, even when bosses appear to strive to make up for their bad behaviors. **Sanctions, rather than forgiveness, are more likely to change behaviors.**

Here's a list of strategies to use with leaders who have Anti-Social Personality Disorders (APD)

1. **Recognize the signs of leaders with Anti-Social Personality Disorders**

Psychopaths are more deceptive and manipulative and maintain more control over their outward personas. They are able to lead what appear to be normal lives, sometimes throughout their lifetime. When psychopaths become criminals they believe they are smarter than the average person and invincible. Sociopaths often let their inner rage surface with violent episodes, verbally and physically. They become reckless and spontaneous and have little control over what they say or how they act.

Because they are impulse driven, they rarely consider the consequences of their actions. It is difficult for sociopaths to live normal lives, and because of their imprudence many of them drop out of school, can't hold jobs, turn to crime, and end up in prison. Psychopaths have delusions of grandeur, lack remorse, empathy or guilt, and have very shallow emotions and like sociopaths, lack a sense of responsibility. Sociopaths lack empathy for others; have difficulty forming relationships; are manipulative and deceitful and are impulsive and irresponsible. In the case of a narcissistic bosses, they exaggerate their own IQ, success or looks, lack empathy, and have a sense of entitlement. All three of these personality types are extremely manipulative and dishonest.

2. Adjust Your Communication Style

This could involve several actions. For some it means cutting off all contact, or keeping it to a bare minimum. For others, it could mean continuing to talk to them, but simply keeping your guard up. Limit the conversations to the specific business at hand and do not have conversations about your personal life or other people.

3. Don't divulge anything personal

Keep all your important, confidential information close to you. Don't let them know anything that could be used against you, and definitely don't go too far in depth about future plans or long-term desires and wishes. Do not socialize with them.

4. Refrain from feeling indebted

If you get too invested in a leader who exhibits anti-social personality disorder (APD) behavior, it could be dangerous for you in the end. They often ask you to do favors normal people wouldn't, sometimes putting you in risky situations where you're unable to uphold your own moral beliefs. If you do find yourself falling in too deep, seek professional help. It might be your only way out.

5. Don't believe anything you can't independently corroborate.

Operate with the understanding you can't believe anything a corporate APD says. Because of this, continually gather information you'll need to assess what's going on. Be seen as a confidant within the organization. Ask open-ended questions, listen, and observe what's actually happening.

6. Minimize one-off conversations and avoid decisions during them.

If you're working with a corporate APD, to the extent you can, use one-on-one conversations to ask questions and engage in harmless small talk which may help you better understand the individual. Avoid using one-on-one conversations as decision making opportunities because you want witnesses for the decisions a corporate sociopath makes. Push decision making to meetings where others are present who can corroborate decisions and direction setting when they've inevitably changed later.

7. Continually hone your flexibility and scenario planning skills.

When corporate APDs try in some unanticipated way to disrupt efforts where you're making progress, you want to be able to adapt and keep going as readily as possible. It's critical to do the strategic thinking that allows you to stay several steps ahead at all times.

8. Make smart trade-offs to keep the corporate APD placated and occupied.

If your boss is the offender, you can't play the "avoid" and "small talk" cards all the time. Decipher what's important and what isn't to the organization – not to the corporate APD. With that insight, placate sociopaths on all minor things you can to ideally buy a little room for quiet defiance on things that really do count. If you're in a position to do it, pair a lower impact team member with the APD to provide attention and crank through the busywork APDs create. In exchange, offer strong support and counsel to the person assigned to this role.

9. Carefully identify others who understand there's a problem person in your midst.

Be on the lookout for others who hint at frustration or exasperation with a corporate APD. Probe, without saying or revealing anything self-incriminating, and see where their loyalties are and what perspectives they'll express. It may be someone you can work with more closely to get things accomplished. Again, be careful it's someone you can ABSOLUTELY trust.

10. Never depending on a corporate APD to do real work.

Cover your bases by minimizing any dependencies on them completing tasks. If they do own a task, figure out how to make sure someone else is backing them up, so that the APD can't blame you for incompletion.

11. Ensure your actions or behavior don't in any way participate in or support the unethical behavior.

APDs like to draw others into their unethical behavior, partly so they can allocate blame to someone else if they are caught or called to task.

12. Don't think you can outsmart a psychopathic leader.

As smart and experienced as you think you are, or convinced others have your back if there's a conflict, remember that the psychopathic leader eats breakfast, lunch and dinner thinking about ways he can screw the organization and the people in it, and ways to avoid detection, blame or consequences.

If the organization has whistle-blower policies and procedures use them. Consider contacting legal authorities if the transgression is significant. Consult with a labor relations legal expert or lawyer to seek advice. Exercise extreme caution about casually discussing your suspicions with others.

Harvard University Psychologist and author of *The Sociopath in The Office Next Door*, Martha Stout, suggests the following strategies:

- **Trust your instincts.** Martha Stout's research shows that statistically, the odds you are dealing with a sociopath are higher than you may think. When a boss starts to publicly castigate you (or others) for mistakes you didn't actually make, take note. When joking becomes sarcastic, one or two individuals are perpetually targeted, or a boss maliciously plays team members against each other, there may be a deeper issue at play. Take notes, and proceed with caution.

- **Keep Records.** Ask questions that clarify the behavior you suspect. A true APD generally operates one on one, and thrives on situations they can turn into a "he said/she said" scenario after the fact. To the extent you can document instructions and commitments in email (or even through recordings, if you are careful) you will be further ahead.

- **Call the person out and defend yourself (carefully).** If you can do so calmly and without losing your temper, stop the meeting, stop the discussion, set a one-on-one appointment with the individual in question, and do whatever else is necessary to hold your ground and avoid becoming a pawn. This will send the message that you're not a victim to be played or walked over. **Proceed with care**—the effort to defend yourself could backfire if it makes you an even bigger target, or allows a mean-spirited boss to view you (or paint you) as disrespectful or uncooperative—but ultimately, you will be better off for having carefully defended the boundary that you are not willing to be treated unfairly or "played".

(A footnote: This strategy does not work with a psychopath. You take an enormous risk in calling out or confronting the psychopath. It's a contest you can't win.)

- **Never, never trust that person again.** Sociopaths are a breed of leopards that will not (and cannot) change their spots. They may be smooth and persuasive; they may promise you anything—but once a person like this has been unveiled, avoid at all costs any scenario that forces you to work with them again.

- **Leave.** If the organization is unable or unwilling to deal with the situation, your only hope is to leave. This is a scenario that occurs with surprising frequency—it is hard for an organization to fathom that a single individual could be at the core of so much harm, or the company may fear the repercussions of firing a person whose propensity for sabotage is known to be strong. In any case, if the company is unwilling to deal with the individual directly, your most productive choice will likely be to leave.

Advice if You Are Dealing with a Leader with a Narcissistic Personality Disorder

Attempts to change their behavior toward you, by standard methods such as telling them how their behavior makes you feel, will not work. In general, trying to change the behavior of narcissistic will primarily lead to frustration. It is best to accept that they were so damaged in their emotional development that they lack the ability to empathize and behave reasonably. Keeping this in mind will help you avoid taking their criticism personally or arguing with them about it. Disagreeing with their critical statements will only enrage them.

- First and foremost, abandon the idea that you will be able to change the leader to become humble, honest and ethical. Even psychotherapists have limited success.

- Avoid gossiping with other leaders or managers in the organization, borrowing from them, or lending to them. It makes you vulnerable.

- Document, document, document. Narcissistic leaders like to both use verbal conversations and "code" language that can be vague or debatable. This allows the narcissist to deny agreements or responsibility and also "gaslight" others.

- Be empathetic to a point, and don't be sympathetic. The narcissist will see this a weakness and try to exploit it.

- Do not confront the narcissistic leader in private or especially in front of others. They will exact revenge on you. If the behavior is serious enough to report it, do so to the leader's superiors when you leave the organization. Even reporting it to the leader's boss while you remain in the organization is a risk, because you don't know the nature of the relationship between the narcissistic leader and his boss.

- Go with the flow and be complimentary at first. Pay attention to the leader's schema, or "mental model of aspects of the world or of the self that is structured in such a way as to facilitate the processes of cognition and perception"; again, they'll usually pertain to one or more of the following themes: strength, intelligence, talent, social class, beauty, and/or money. Then, praise them for accomplishments in those areas where you feel comfortable (without encouraging superficiality or bad behavior).

- Provide feedback but not criticism. This is a delicate balance. Narcissists will react negatively to any criticism and actually act vengefully. Be sure your language is specific and cites behavior that is being repeated over time.

- Note the narcissist's triggers which the leader could interpret as blows to their ego and avoid those triggers.

- Maintain assertive personal boundaries. Trying to have a friendship or close relationship with a narcissist is not a good idea. Remember they can turn on you on a dime.

Finally, the best advice I can give if you are dealing with a boss who is has a narcissistic personality disorder (NPD) is get out of the organization as soon as you can.

CHAPTER 9

How to Develop Moral, Ethical and Wise Leaders

"Strong ethics keep corporations healthy. Poor ethics make companies sick. Values are the immune system of every organization."

Patrick Dixon

E ven in the best of times, government corruption and mismanagement are harmful – they can cost lives and financial resources. In today's pandemic they fuel a spiraling tragedy. Together, they will prolong the crisis by undermining government efficiency, significantly increasing the loss of life, wasting untold resources, and reducing society's already fragile trust in government – each of which has significant long-term consequences that will linger far longer than the virus itself.

As the COVID-19 pandemic – perhaps the greatest challenge to governments in our lifetime – mounts, we must build a coalition of civil society, business leaders, dedicated government officials and funders to strengthen government accountability and effectiveness and change the trajectory of this pandemic and our futures. Here's how.

Robert Chesnut is a Silicon Valley expert and the Chief Ethics Officer of Airbnb Inc., his new book, *Intentional Integrity: How Smart Companies Can Lead an Ethical Revolution,* describes how today's headlines are filled with stories of bad behavior by companies and leaders—sexual harassment, fraud, conflicts of interest, privacy violations, anti-competitive behavior, and more.

This is partly because consumers, employees, and the press are all more empowered now than ever; employees can share information instantly through apps like Slack, and if their company's values don't align with their personal values, they may walk out—or become the next whistleblower, and take a CEO down with them.

Companies that don't see the integrity revolution coming are going to be vulnerable, but companies that know the revolution is here are poised to make integrity a superpower that can energize their employees, inspire their customers, and earn the respect of partners, governments, and the world at large.

Chesnut argues that for much of the 20th century, companies were focused on profit, revenue, and driving shareholder value. Integrity has become compliance, simply something that you have to get through because it's legally required. But those actions don't inspire or motivate people, because they realize that those materials were produced by somebody else, for somebody else. Instead, corporate integrity is a muscle that companies must learn to exercise intentionally.

He goes on to say that to build integrity in a company, we just have to weed out the bad actors. Behavioral psychologists have demonstrated that when you place human beings in an environment where they have even a small incentive to lie, a large number of people, 70% or more, will fudge the truth for their own benefit. On the other hand, if you are consistently reminded of your better self, if the people around you talk about doing what is right, and if leaders in particular are acting with integrity, then you are far more likely to act with integrity yourself.

Chesnut proposes Six C's to foster corporate integrity:

- The first C stands for **Chief Executive Officer**, because it all starts at the top. If the company has no noble purpose that leadership is committed to following, then any effort at integrity will almost certainly fail.

- The second C stands for a **Customized Code of Ethics**. You can't take someone else's code of ethics, slap your name on it, and call it your own; you need something specific and appropriate for your company.

- The third C is for **Communicating the Code**, because employees want to hear how their new company is committed to values that align with their own.

- The fourth C is a **Clear Reporting System**. You have to tell employees that you really do want to hear when problems arise, and you need a system that makes everyone feel comfortable coming forward with their concerns.

- The fifth C is **Consequences**—show that you're committed to following through when even a senior-level employee breaks the rules.

- And finally, the sixth C is **Constant**. Keeping a constant flow of communication about the importance of integrity is critical to building that environment that feeds the good wolf in all.

Demand greater accountability

Following the maxim "we get the government we deserve", we need to unite citizens to press for greater accountability and effectiveness from government institutions. This has already started as civil society organizations are building coalitions to hold government to account and defend government whistleblowers. Coalitions of NGOs are calling on the US Congress and the International Monetary Fund to include anti-corruption safeguards in all emergency pandemic funding.

The Coronavirus Facts Database has fact-checkers in more than 70 countries monitoring pandemic mis/disinformation, while the Accountability Lab's Coronavirus CivActs Campaign is debunking rumors and helping governments around the world deliver reliable public health information.

Organizations like Represent Us are helping pass anti-corruption measures in states and cities across the US. In Europe, citizens in the Czech Republic and Poland joined large anti-corruption demonstrations last year and a newly created European Public Prosecutor's Office, due to launch later this year, will have extensive powers to investigate and prosecute the misuse of EU funds. Meanwhile, organizations like Transparency International, Open Society Foundations, and the Group of States against Corruption, the Council of Europe's anti-corruption body, continue to press for reforms.

Business leaders must also commit to fair dealing and must exhibit transparency and accountability – and not just because, as the National Law Review warned, failing to do so carries a reputational risk. Businesses should join civil society's call for greater accountability from governments because they too must live with the consequences should governments fail.

Leadership Now, a group of US business leaders, has put together a primer for business on how to help improve government performance and restore trust. The B Team, a group of global business leaders forging a more responsible approach to capitalism, has called for companies to counter government violations of human rights in response to the pandemic.

During this crisis, which presents seemingly endless opportunities for self-dealing, malfeasance and plain-old misjudgments, dedicated public servants around the world should find allies and resources through organizations like the Open Government Partnership, which has developed a guide for open government reformers and a list of more than 200 crowd sourced examples of practical ideas, tools and resources on how civil servants can fulfil their duties more effectively and transparently.

In the midst of this pandemic-induced government spending spree, the open contracting community has recommendations on how governments can buy emergency equipment fast and without favor. The Council of Europe's anti-corruption monitoring body, meanwhile, has issued guidelines for public servants in its member states to mitigate humankind's worst inclinations.

Finally, funders must recognize this as a moment to pivot from retail philanthropy towards catalytic philanthropy. Do the math; philanthropy's response to the pandemic will be measured in the billions of dollars, while governments' responses will be in the trillions.

To maximize impact, a good portion of philanthropy's billions should be directed at ensuring the much larger government response is effective and that government systems are strengthened for the long term. The Chandler Foundation responded to the crisis by joining the donor collaborative Transparency and Accountability Initiative (TAI), which offers tools to help funders support good governance. Another donor collaborative, Co-Impact, invests in organizations working to improve government accountability, efficiency and effectiveness – partnerships that have never been more critical.

Guiding Principles for Moral, Ethical and Wise Leadership

Here are some more suggestions on how society in general and organizations specifically can emphasize to a greater degree guiding principles for moral, ethical and wise behavior, with a focus on leaders.

- Place an emphasis on integrity in behaviors—demand it of ourselves and those who we work with and lead us.

- Stop recruiting overconfident, narcissistic and sociopathic/psychopathic people for leadership positions in our institutions and organizations, and opt instead for the honest, humble and compassionate leaders.

- Recruit and promote more women into leadership positions. Research has shown that female leaders are less prone to corrupt and unethical behavior.

- Engage in a serious overhaul of the current capitalistic system which has a structure and practices that facilitate amoral and unethical behavior, and unwise decisions to the detriment of the populace and the planet. In particular, shareholder interests as the primary driver for business decisions must be abandoned. Encourage business organizations to complete a serious overhaul of their current ethical principles and policies.

- Encourage business schools to put more emphasis on the study of humanities including philosophy and ethics; provide more support for the humanities in post secondary education rather than the current emphasis on technical knowledge and expertise in business.

- Encourage business leaders (and their employees) to become more involved in worthy causes that benefit society and the planet that are not tied to economic or financial gain.

- Enact stronger laws, policies, regulations and procedures to protect whistle blowers who witness or encounter unethical (or amoral) organizational practices.

- Emphasize the importance of developing self-awareness and emotional intelligence in leadership development programs and training.

- Encourage leader practices that promote exposure to various forms of ethnic and cultural (and gender) diversity.

- Encourage the public school system to include in both teacher training and curriculum the teaching of civics, moral and ethical behavior, critical thinking and Socratic dialogue.

- Encourage the public school system to initiate curriculum and practical experiences for students aimed at social good and environmental protection.

- Engage in "good conversations" about moral values, and ethical behavior.

- Exposure to the complexity of whole systems, rather than only discrete small parts or functional area.

- Study significant issues from an integrated perspective rather than a narrow perspective.

- Work collaboratively with others on significant problems or challenges that impact the welfare of all.

- Develop excellence in listening and perspective-taking.

- Work as a volunteer on an issue or project that benefits others, humanity and/or the planet without the need for recognition or compensation.

- Actively engage in the responsibilities of being a citizen in a democracy.

- Be an advocate for justice and fairness for all.

AFTERWORD

R ecent events have brought into clear focus that we are at a turning point in our democracies which exposes the real dangers to their continued existence.

The corruption of the Trump presidency, the viral spread of deliberate disinformation and lies by politicians and business leaders at all levels, and the rampant vitriolic and destructive use of social media platforms have all underscored how morality and ethics have declined and are under siege in the world, and sadly, America.

We are at a watershed and tipping point in human history. The viability of democratic institutions, the health and welfare of people and our planet now requires dramatic individual and collective action to be led by moral, ethical and wise leaders.

The choice we make could spell ongoing chaos and disasters or bold new action. Ignorance and rose colored glasses, hopeful wishes and prayers will not be enough. The time for individual and collective action is now.

REFERENCES

Akers, J. (1989). ``Ethics and competitiveness putting first things first''. *Sloan Management Review*, 30(2), 69-76.

Alford, H. (2010). The practical wisdom of "personalism". *Journal of Management Development*, 29(7/8), 697–705.

Alzola, M. (2015). Virtuous persons and virtuous actions in business ethics and organizational research. *Business Ethics Quarterly*, 25(3), 287–318.

Ardelt, M. (1997). Wisdom and life satisfaction in old age. *Journal of Gerontology*, 52, 15–27.

Arlin, P. K. (1990). Wisdom: The art of problem finding. In R. J. Sternberg (Ed.), *Wisdom: Its Nature Origins, and Development* (pp. 230–243). New York: Cambridge University Press.

Argandon, A. (2015). Humility in management. *Journal of Business Ethics*, 132(1), 63–71.

Ashford, S. (1989). Self-assessments in organizations: A literature review and integrative model. *Research in Organizational Behavior*, 11, 133-74.

Ashforth, B. E. (1994). Petty tyranny in organizations. *Human Relations*, 47: 755-79.

Assmann, A. (1994). Wholesome knowledge: Concepts of wisdom in a historical and cross-cultural perspective. In

D. L. Featherman, R. M. Learner, & M. Perlmutter. (Eds.), *Life-span Development and Behavior* (pp. 187–224). Hillsdale, NJ: Lawrence Erlbaum.

Bachmann, C. (2014). Can practical wisdom be taught in business schools? An inquiry-based learning approach for management education. In P. Blessinger & J. M. Carfora (Eds*.), Inquiry-Based Learning for the Arts, Humanities, and Social Sciences: A Conceptual and Practical Resource for Educators.* Bradford, England: Emerald Group Publishing.

Badaracco, J. (2006). *Questions of Character: Illuminating the Heart of Leadership Through Literature.* Boston: Harvard Business School Press.

Badaracco, J. L. (1997). *Defining Moments: When Managers Must Choose Between Right and Right.* Boston: Harvard Business School Press.

Badaracco, J. L., & Webb, A. (1995). Business ethics: A view from the trenches. *California Management Review, 37,* 8-8.

Baltes, P. B., & Kunzmann, U. (2003). Wisdom. *The Psychologist,* 16(3), 131–133.

Baltes, P. B., & Smith, J. (1990). Toward a psychology of wisdom and its ontogenesis. In J. R. Sternberg (Ed.), *Wisdom: Its Nature, Origins, and Development* (pp. 87–120). New York: Cambridge University Press.

Bartunek, J. M., & Trullen, J. (2007). Individual ethics — the virtue of prudence. In E. H. Kessler & J. R. Bailey (Eds.),

Handbook of Organizational and Managerial Wisdom (pp. 91–107). Thousand Oaks, CA: Sage Publications.

Bass, B. M., & Steidlmeier, P. (1999). Ethics, character, and authentic transformational leadership behavior. *Leadership Quarterly*, 10, 181-218.

Bazerman, M. H. (2008). Evaluating Your Business Ethics: A Harvard professor explains why good people do unethical things. *Gallup Management Journal Online* (pp. 1-5): Gallup Poll News Service.

Baumhart, R. C. (1991). How ethical are businessmen? *Harvard Business Review*, 39, 6-8.

Beabout, G. (2013). *The Character of the Manager: From Office Executive to Wise Steward*. New York: Springer.

Burns, J. M. (2014). Foreword. In J. B. Ciulla (Ed.), *Ethics, the Heart of Leadership* (3rd Ed.). (pp. ix–xii). Santa Barbara: Praeger.

Beekun, R. I. (2012). Character centered leadership: Muhammad as an ethical role model for CEOs. *Journal of Management Development*, 31(10), 1003–1020.

Ben-Hur, S., & Jonsen, K. (2012). Ethical leadership: Lessons from Moses. *Journal of Management Development*, 31(9), 962–973.

Bennis, W. G., & O'Toole, J. (2005). How business schools lost their way. *Harvard Business Review*, 83(5), 96–104.

Beyer, J. M., & Nino, D. (1998). Facing the future: Backing courage with wisdom. In S. Srivastva & D. L. Cooperrider (Eds.), *Organizational Wisdom and Executive Courage* (pp. 65–97). San Francisco: New Lexington Press.

Biloslavo, R., & McKenna, B. (2013). Evaluating the process of wisdom in wise political leaders using a developmental wisdom model. In W. Kü¨pers & D. J. Pauleen (Eds.), *A Handbook of Practical Wisdom: Leadership, Organization and Integral Business Practice* (pp. 111–132). Farnham, MA.: Gower.

Bird, F. B. (1996). *The Muted Conscience: Moral Silence and the Practice of Ethics in Business*. Westport, CT: Quorum Books.

Bird, F. B., & Waters, J. A. (1987). The nature of managerial moral standards. *Journal of Business Ethics*, 6(1), 1–13.

Bird, F. B., & Waters, J. A. (1989). The moral muteness of managers. *California Management Review*, 32(1), 73–88.

Bird, F. B., Westley, F., & Waters, J. A. (1989). The uses of moral talk: Why do managers talk ethics. *Journal of Business Ethics*, 8(1), 75–89.

Blanchard, K. H., & Peale, N. V. (1996). *The Power of Ethical Management*. New York, N.Y.: Ballantine Books.

Bright, D. S., Winn, B. A., & Kanov, J. (2014). Reconsidering virtue: Differences of perspective in virtue ethics and the positive social sciences. *Journal of Business Ethics*, 119(4), 445–460.

Brenner, S. N., & Molander, E. A. (1977). Is the ethics of business changing? *Harvard Business Review,* 55: 57-71.

Brief, A. P., Buttram, R. T., & Dukerich, J. M. (2001). Collective corruption in the corporate world: Toward a process model. **In** M. E. Turner (Ed.), *Groups at work: Theory and Research, pp.* 471-99.

Brief, A. P., Dukerich, J. M., & Doran, L. J. (1991). Resolving ethical dilemmas in management: Experimental investigations of values, accountability, and choice. *Journal of Applied Social Psychology,* 21, 380-96.

Brown, M. E., & Trevino, L. K. (2006). Ethical leadership: A review and future directions. *Leadership Quarterly,* 17(6), 595–616.

Brown, M. E. (2007). Misconceptions of ethical leadership: How to avoid potential pitfalls. *Organizational Dynamics,* 3, 140-55.

Brown, M. E., Treviño, L. K., & Harrison, D. A. (2005). Ethical leadership: A social learning perspective for construct development and testing. *Organizational Behavior and Human Decision Processes,* 97, 117-34.

Butterfield, K. D., Trevino, L. K., & Weaver, G. R. (2000). Moral awareness in business organizations: Influences of issue-related and social context factors. *Human Relations,* 53(7), 981–1018.

Carsten, M. K., & Uhl-Bien, M. (2013). Ethical Followership: An examination of followership beliefs and crimes of obedience. *Journal of Leadership & Organizational Studies*, 20(1), 49–61.

Chen, S. (2010). Bolstering unethical leaders: the role of the media, financial analysts and shareholders. *Journal of Public Affairs*, 10, 200-215.

Ciulla, J. B. (1995). Leadership ethics: Mapping the territory. *Business Ethics Quarterly*, 5(1), 5–28.

Ciulla, J. B. (2005). The state of leadership ethics and the work that lies before us. *Business Ethics: A European Review*, 14(4), 323–335.

Ciulla, J. B. (Ed.). (2014). *Ethics, the heart of leadership* (3rd Ed.). Santa Barbara: Praeger.

Ciulla, J. B. (2014). Habits and virtues: Does it matter if a leader kicks a dog? *Rivista Internazionale Di Filosofia E Psicologia*, 5(3), 332–342.

Ciulla, J. B., Knights, D., Mabey, C., & Tomkins, L. (2018). Philosophical contributions to leadership ethics. *Business Ethics Quarterly*, 28(1), 1–14.

Crosbie, R. (2008). Who defines ethics in your organization? *Industrial and Commercial Training*, 40(4), 181–187.

Csikszentmihalyi, M., & Rathunde, K. (1990). The psychology of wisdom: An evolutionary interpretation. In R. J. Sternberg (Ed.), *Wisdom: Its Nature, Origins and Development*, Cambridge: Cambridge University Press, pp.25–51.

De Hoogh, A. H. B., & Den Hartog, D. N. (2008). Ethical and despotic leadership, relationships with leader's social responsibility, top management team effectiveness and subordinates' optimism: A multi-method study. *Leadership Quarterly*, 19, 297-311.

Detert, J. R., Treviño, L. K., & Sweitzer, V. L. (2008). Moral disengagement in ethical decision making: A study of antecedents and outcomes. *Journal of Applied Psychology*, 93, 374-91.

Deslandes, G. (2012). Power, profits, and practical wisdom: Ricoeur's perspectives on the possibility of ethics in institutions. *Business and Professional Ethics Journal*, 31(1), 1–24.

Dobos, N., Barry, C., & Pogge, T. (2011). *Global Financial Crisis: The Ethical Issues*. New York: Palgrave Macmillan.

Dolan, S. L., Garcia, S., & Richley, B. (2006). *Managing by values; A Corporate Guide to Living, Being Alive and Making a Living in the 21st Century*. New York: Palgrave Macmillian.

Duffy, J. (2012). The conscience of an organization: the ethics office. *Strategy & Leadership*, 28(3), 17–21.

Freeman, R. E., Dunham, L., & Mc Vea, J. (2007). Strategic ethics— strategy, wisdom and stakeholder theory: A pragmatic and entrepreneurial view of stakeholder strategy. In E. H. Kessler & J. R. Bailey (Eds.), *Handbook of Organizational and Managerial Wisdom* (pp. 151–180). Thousand Oaks, CA: Sage.

143

Gellerman, S. W. (1989). Managing ethics from the top down. *Sloan Management Review,* 30(2), 73-79.

Gibson, P. S. (2008). Developing practical management wisdom. *Journal of Management Development,* 27(5), 528–536.

Glück, J.; König, S., Naschenweng, K., Redzanowski, U., Dorner-Hörig, L., Straßer, I, Wiedermann, W. (2013). How to measure wisdom: Content, reliability, and validity of five measures. *Frontiers in Psychology,* 4, 405.

Gluck, J., Bluck, S., Baron, J., & McAdams, D. P. (2005). The wisdom of experience: Autobiographical narratives across adulthood. *International Journal of Behavioral Development,* 29(3), 197–208.

Grojean, M. W., Resick, C. J., Dickson, M. W., & Smith, D. B. (2004). Leaders, values, and organizational climate: Examining leadership strategies for establishing an organizational climate regarding ethics. *Journal of Business Ethics,* 55(3), 223–241.

Intezari, A., & Pauleen, D. J. (2014). Management wisdom in perspective: Are you virtuous enough to succeed in volatile times? *Journal of Business Ethics,* 120(3), 393–404.

Jeannot, T. M. (1989). Moral leadership and practical wisdom. *International Journal of Social Economics,* 16(6), 14–38.

Jones, C. A. (2005). Wisdom Paradigms for the enhancement of ethical and profitable business practices. *Journal of Business Ethics*, 57(4), 363–375.

Jordan, J., Brown, M. E., & Treviño, L. K., 2010. The executive as ethical leader: The relationship between leader-follower ethical reasoning and perceived ethical leadership. University of Groningen. Unpublished manuscript.

Kahneman, D., & Tversky, A. 1979. Prospect theory: An analysis of decisions under risk. *Econometrica*, 47, 263-91.

Kanungo, R., & Mendonca, M. (1996). *Ethical dimensions of leadership*. Thousand Oaks, CA: Sage.

Ku¨pers, W. M., & Pauleen, D. J. (2013). *A Handbook of Practical Wisdom. Leadership, Organization and Integral Business Practice*. Surrey, England: Gower Publishing.

Mayer, D. M., Kuenzi, M., Greenbaum, R., Bardes, M., & Salvador, R. (2009). How low does ethical leadership now? Test of a trickle-down model. *Organizational Behavior and Human Decision Processes*, 108, 1-13.

Munro, I., & Thanem, T. (2018). The ethics of affective leadership: Organizing good encounters without leaders. *Business Ethics Quarterly*, 28(1), 717–734.

Neuter, M. J., Carlson, D, S, Kalmar, K. M., Roberts, J. A., & Chunk, L. B. 2009, The virtuous influence of ethical leadership behavior: Evidence from the field. *Journal of Business Ethics*, 90, 157-70.

Proves, C. (2010). Virtuous decision making for business ethics. *Journal of Business Ethics*, 91(1), 3–16.

Cruzan, P., & Cruzan Michelson, K. (2007). *Leading with Wisdom*. Sheffield: Greenleaf Publishing.

Pasupathi, M. and U.M. Staudinger. (2001). Do advanced moral reasoners also show wisdom? Linking moral reasoning and wisdom-related knowledge and judgment. *International Journal of Behavioral Development*.

Pelletier, K. L., & Bligh, M. C. (2008). The aftermath of organizational corruption: Employee attributions and emotional reactions. *Journal of Business Ethics*, 80, 823-44.

Piccolo, R, F., Greenbaum, R., Den Hartog, D. N., & Folger, R., (2010). The relationship between ethical leadership and core job characteristics. *Journal of Organizational Behavior, 31, 259-78.*

Pinto, J., Leana, C. R., & Pil, F. K. (2008). Corrupt organizations or organizations of corrupt individuals? Two types of organization-level corruption. *Academy of Management Review,* 33, 685-709.

Podsakoff, P. M., MacKenzie, S. B., Moorman, R. H., & Fetter, R. (1990). Transformational leader behaviors and their effects on followers' trust in leader, satisfaction, and organizational citizenship behaviors. *Leadership Quarterly,* 1, 107-42.

Resick, C, Hanges, P., Dickson, M., & Mitchelson, J. (2006). A cross-cultural examination of the endorsement of ethical leadership. *Journal of Business Ethics, 63,* 345-59.

Rubin, **R.** S., Dierdorff, E. C, & Brown, M. E. (2010). Do ethical leaders get ahead? Exploring ethical leadership and promotability. *Business Ethics Quarterly,* 20, 215-36.

Salvador, R., & Folger, R. 2009. Business ethics and the brain. *Business Ethics Quarterly, 19,* 1-31.

Schminke, M., Ambrose, M. L., & Neubaum, D. O. (2005). The effect of leader moral development on ethical climate and employee attitudes. *Organizational Behavior and Human Decision Processes, 97,* 135-51.

Schminke, M., Wells, D., Peyreffite, J., & Sebora, T. C. (2002). Leadership and ethics in work groups: A longitudinal assessment. *Group and Organization Management,* 27, 272-93.

Schwartz, M. S. (2002). A code of ethics for corporate code of ethics. *Journal of Business Ethics,* 41(1–2), 27–43.

Sherman, N. (2000). Wise emotions. In W. S. Brown (Ed.), *Understanding Wisdom: Sources, Science and Society* (pp. 319–338). Radnor: Templeton Foundation Press.

Sims, R. R. (1992). The challenge of ethical behavior in organizations. *Journal of Business Ethics,* 11(7), 505-513.

Sison, A. J. G. (2003). *The Moral Capital of Leaders: Why Virtue Matters.* Cheltenham, England: Edward Elgar Publishing Limited.

Sison, A. J. G., Hartman, E. M., & Fontrodona, J. (2012). Reviving tradition: Virtue and the common good in business and management. *Business Ethics Quarterly*, 22(2), 207–210.

Sternberg, R. J. (1990). Understanding wisdom. In R. Sternberg (Ed.), *Wisdom, Intelligence and Creativity Synthesized* (pp. 3 -9). New York, NY: Cambridge University Press.

Swanton, C. (2003). *Virtue Ethics: A Pluralistic View.* Oxford: Oxford University Press.

Takahashi, M., & Bordia, P. (2000). The concept of wisdom: A crosscultural comparison. *International Journal of Psychology*, 35(1), 1–9.

Takahashi, Masami and Willis F. Overton. (2002). Wisdom: A culturally inclusive developmental perspective. *International Journal of Behavioral Development*, 6, 34-44.

Thomas, T., Schermerhorn, J. R., & Dienhart, J. W. (2004). Strategic leadership of ethical behavior in business. *Academy of Management Executive*, 18, 56-66.

Toor, S., & Ofori, G. (2009). Ethical leadership: Examining the relationships with full range leadership model, employee outcomes, and organizational culture. *Journal of Business Ethics*, 90, 533-47.

Treviño, L. K. 1986. Ethical decision making in organizations: A person-situation interactionist model. *Academy of Management Review,* 11, 601-17.

Treviño, L. K., Brown, M., & Hartman, L. P. (2003). A qualitative investigation of perceived executive ethical leadership: Perceptions from inside and outside the executive suite. *Human Relations,* 55, 5-37.

Treviño, L. K., Hartman, L. P., & Brown, M. (2000). Moral person and moral manager: How executive develop a reputation for ethical leadership. *California Management Review,* 42, 128-132.

Treviño, L. K., Weaver, G. R., & Reynolds, S. J. (2006.) Behavioral ethics in organizations: A review. *Journal of Management,* 32, 951-90.

Waddock, S. (2010). Finding wisdom within—the role of seeing and reflective practice in developing moral imagination, aesthetic sensibility, and systems understanding. *Journal of Business Ethics Education,* 7, 177–196.

Waddock, S. (2014). Wisdom and responsible leadership: Aesthetic sensibility, moral imagination, and systems thinking. In D. Koehn & D. Elm (Eds.), *Aesthetics and Business Ethics* (pp. 29–147). Dordrecht, NL: Springer.

Walumbwa, F. O., & Schaubroeck, J. (2009). Leader personality traits and employee voice behavior: Mediating roles of ethical leadership and work group psychological safety. *Journal of Applied Psychology,* 94, 1275-86.

Weaver, G. R., and Brown, M. E. In press. Moral foundations at work: new factors to consider in understanding the nature and role of ethics in organizations. In A. Tenbrunsel & D. De Cremer (Eds.), *Behavioral Business Ethics: Ideas on an Emerging Field. New York:* Psychology Press.

Weaver, G. R., Treviño, L. K., & Cochran, P. L. (1999). Corporate ethics programs as control systems: Influences of executive commitment and environmental factors. *Academy of Management Journal,* 42, 41-57.

W. Ku¨pers & D. J. Pauleen. (2001). *A Handbook of Practical Wisdom: Leadership, Organization and Integral Business Practice* (pp. 111–132). Farnham, England: Gower.

Yang, S.-Y. (2011). Wisdom displayed through leadership: Exploring leadership-related wisdom. *The Leadership Quarterly,* 22(4), 616–632.

Other Books by Ray Williams

I Know Myself and Neither Do You: Why Charisma, Confidence and Pedigree Won't Take You Where You Want to Go

Eye of the Storm: How Mindful Leaders Can Transform Chaotic Workplaces

The Leadership Edge: Strategies to Transform School Systems

Dragon Tamer

Ready, Aim, Influence (contributing author)

Systemic Change: Touchstones for the Future School (contributing author)

About the Author

RAY WILLIAMS provides executive coaching, speaking and professional consultations services worldwide. He has over 35 years' experience as a Superintendent of Schools, CEO, senior HR executive, management consultant, trainer, executive coach, professional speaker and author. He has received his undergraduate and graduate training in History, English, Psychology and Organizational Leadership. He is a Certified Master Executive Coach and Certified Hypnotherapist.

He is currently President and CEO of Ray Williams Associates, an executive coaching firm based in Vancouver, providing coaching and mentoring to executives in the public and private sectors worldwide. He also is an associate of ViRTUS Inc., a leadership development company based in Vancouver.

He is past president of the International Coach Federation in Vancouver, and held several board positions professional associations in North America. In addition, he has served as a director and Vice-Chair for the Vancouver Board of Trade and director for several community organizations.

His clients have included Fortune 500 companies, the Best Managed Companies in Canada, and dozens of small businesses and entrepreneurial start-ups. He has been recognized as one of the top C-Suite coaches in Canada.

He has written extensively about leadership, the workplace, organizations, personal development, and social issues including two books on leadership; contributed to several books organizational issues; a novel and screenplay; and been interviewed by or written articles for national publications and the media such as *The Financial Post, The Washington Post, Entrepreneur, The Globe and Mail, the Vancouver Sun, USA Today and Inc., and online media such as Psychology Today, Fulfillment Daily, Business.com and Medium.* He has written two books on leadership, *The Leadership Edge,* and was a contributing author to *Ready, Aim, Influence.* In addition, he has written a novel, *Dragon Tamer.*

His latest books are: *I Know Myself and Neither Do You: Why Charisma, Confidence and Pedigree Won't Take You Where You Want to Go,* which examines the research and practices of self-awareness as the key to great leadership, and *Eye of the Storm: How Mindful Leaders Can Transform Chaotic Workplaces,* which looks at how mindful leaders can make a big difference to organizational success and employee well being.

Beyond his professional training and experience, he brings his insights into human behavior, having been born and raised in Hong Kong, where his family was imprisoned for four years by the Japanese in WWII, which gives him a unique perspective on overcoming adversity, and sustaining a positive outlook.

About the Author

www.ingramcontent.com/pod-product-compliance
Lightning Source LLC
Chambersburg PA
CBHW070339220526
45467CB00001B/183